KB096643

Vocabulary

TEPS

영어동보카 30일 완성 텝스단어장

발 행 | 2024년 04월 15일
저 자 | David Na
펴낸이 | 한건희
펴낸곳 | 주식회사 부크크
출판사등록 | 2014.07.15(제2014-16호)
주 소 | 서울특별시 금천구 가산디지털1로 119 SK트윈타워 A동 305호
전 화 | 1670-8316
이메일 | info@bookk.co.kr

ISBN | 979-11-410-8091-4

CONTENTS

CONTENTS

*Vocabulary/Expressions   Day 1

abet [əbét]   *vt.* 부추기다, 선동하다
图 assist or encourage, usually in some wrongdoing
图 instigate, encourage, foment, incite, provoke
例 *He abets a me against my boss.*

hazardous [hǽzərdəs]   *a.* 위험한
图 involving risk or danger
图 dangerous, risky, perilous, unsafe, chancy
例 *It is extremely hazardous going out in the tide and fog.*

fixture [fíkstʃər]   *n.* 정착물
图 an object firmly fixed in place especially in a household
图 equipage, furnishing, gear, fitting, appurtenance
例 *kitchen fixtures*

play [pléi]   *vt.* 놀다
图 participate in games or sport
图 perform, act, gambol, rejoice, toy
例 *We played hockey all afternoon.*

advancement [ədvǽnsmənt]   *n.* 진보, 발달
图 gradual improvement or growth or development
图 progress, improvement, development, headway
例 *advancement of knowledge*

construction [kənstrʌ́kʃən]   *n.* 건설
图 the act of building something
图 building, establishment, structure, erection
例 *During the construction we had to take a detour.*

freeway [frí:wèi] · *n.* 고속도로
图 a broad highway designed for high-speed traffic
图 expressway, motorway, speedway, thruway, highway
예 *Go back to the freeway.*

mandatory [mǽndətɔ:ri] · *a.* 강제의
图 required by rule
图 imperative, compulsory, obligatory, requisite, binding
예 *mandatory reading*

raise [reiz] · *vt.* 올리다
图 move from a lower to a higher position
图 lift, boost, elevate, heighten, uplift
예 *Raise your hands.*

grain [gréin] · *n.* 곡물
图 a cereal grass
图 cereal, corn, kernel, seed, granule
예 *Wheat is a grain that is grown in Kansas.*

liberation [lìbəréiʃən] · *n.* 해방, 석방
图 the act of granting freedom to someone or something
图 release, emancipation, disengagement, manumission, enfranchisement
예 *animal liberation*

transform [trænsfɔ:rm] · *vt.* 변형시키다
图 change or alter in form, appearance, or nature
图 convert, transfigure, mutate, metamorphose, transmute, alter
예 *He transformed the clay into a beautiful sculpture.*

imposing [impóuziŋ]   *a.* 인상적인, 훌륭한

图 impressive in appearance

동 magnificent, grand, impressive, majestic, stately

예 *an imposing residence*

---

inhabit [inhǽbit]   *vt.* 살다

图 inhabit or live in

동 reside, abide, dwell, live, populate

예 *The people inhabited the islands that are now deserted.*

---

stock [stάk]   *vt.* 비축하다, 저장하다

图 amass so as to keep for future use or sale or for a particular occasion or use

동 accumulate, store, furnish, provide, supply

예 *Let's stock coffee as long as prices are low.*

---

agriculture [ǽgrikʌltʃər]   *n.* 농업

图 the practice of cultivating the land or raising stock

동 farming, crop production, cultivation, horticulture, agronomy, husbandry

예 *Food and Agriculture Organization*

---

draft [drǽft]   *n.* 밑그림, 초고

图 a preliminary sketch of a design or picture

동 abstract, blueprint, outline, rough drawing, delineation

예 *final draft*

---

escape [iskéip]   *vi.* 도망하다

图 remove oneself from a familiar environment, usually for pleasure or diversion

동 avoid, evade, flee, run, elude

예 *We escaped to our summer house for a few days.*

ingenious [indʒíːnjəs] *a.* 영리한

图 showing inventiveness and skill

동 resourceful, brilliant, clever, inventive, skillful

예 *an ingenious solution to the problem*

---

rush [rʌʃ] *vi.* 돌진하다

图 move fast

동 dash, hurry, run, speed, hasten

예 *He rushed down the hall to receive his guests.*

---

tasty [téisti] *a.* 맛좋은

图 pleasing to the palate

동 appetizing, savory, delicious, palatable, tasteful

예 *a tasty morsel*

---

awful [ɔ́ːfəl] *a.* 무서운

图 causing fear or dread or terror

동 dire, terrible, horrible, dreadful, frightful

예 *the awful war*

---

present [préznt] *vt.* 증정하다

图 give as a present

동 award, furnish, donate, give, offer

예 *What will you present her for her birthday?*

---

consultant [kənsʌ́ltənt] *n.* 상담역

图 an expert who gives advice

동 adviser, tutor, counselor, maven

예 *A consultant helped students select their courses.*

---

interrupt [ìntərʌpt]   *vt.* 방해하다

图 interfere in someone else's activity

图 disturb, interfere, intercept, discontinue, impede

阅 *Please don't interrupt me while I'm on the phone.*

---

disgust [disgʌst]   *vt.* 역겹게 하다

图 cause aversion in

图 abominate, revolt, nauseate, sicken, upset

阅 *This spoilt food disgusts me.*

---

bother [báðər]   *vt.* 괴롭히다

图 cause annoyance in; take the trouble to do something

图 annoy, disturb, plague, vex, molest

阅 *Mosquitoes buzzing in my ear really bothers me.*

---

amusement [əmju:zmənt]   *n.* 즐거움

图 a feeling of delight at being entertained

图 entertainment, fun, pastime, diversion, recreation

阅 *amusement park grounds*

---

physical [fízikəl]   *a.* 육체의, 신체의

图 involving the body as distinguished from the mind or spirit

图 bodily, fleshly, corporal, materialistic

阅 *physical exercise*

---

parentage [péərəntidʒ]   *n.* 태생, 가문, 혈통

图 the descendants of one individual

图 ancestry, bloodline, lineage, pedigree, descent

阅 *His entire parentage has been warriors.*

---

ceremony [serəmouni]   *n.* 의식

图 a formal event performed on a special occasion

图 rite, service, observance, ritual, solemnity

예 *a ceremony commemorating Pearl Harbor*

---

lenient [li:niənt]   *a.* 너그러운

图 tolerant or lenient

图 clement, bland, gentle, indulgent, mild

예 *He is too lenient on the children.*

---

capitalize [kǽpətəlaiz]   *vi.* 이용하다

图 draw advantages from

图 utilize, benefit, obtain, profit, use

예 *He is capitalizing on her mistake.*

---

consumer [kənsu:mər]   *n.* 소비자

图 a person who uses goods or services

图 purchaser, buyer, customer, shopper, user

예 *consumers' price*

---

implementation [impləmənteiʃən]   *n.* 이행

图 the act of accomplishing some aim or executing some order

图 enforcement, accomplishment, execution, fulfilment, realization

예 *The agency was created for the implementation of the policy.*

---

moving [mú:viŋ]   *a.* 움직이는

图 in motion

图 advance, mobile, drive, movable, transfer

예 *the moving parts of the machine*

---

opening [oupəniŋ]   *n.* 틈

图 an open or empty space in or between things

图 crack, gap, hole, space, aperture

예 *There was a small opening between the trees.*

---

dizzy [dízi]   *a.* 현기증나는

图 having or causing a whirling sensation

图 giddy, puzzled, vertiginous, woozy, confused

예 *a dizzy pinnacle*

---

acceptance [ækséptəns]   *n.* 수락

图 the act of receiving what is offered

图 aknowledgement, admission, consent, reception, permission

예 *The organization does not acknowledge this government's acceptance.*

---

stride [stràid]   *vi.* 큰 걸음으로 걷다

图 walk with long steps

图 striddle, march, pace, step, tramp

예 *He strode confidently across the hall.*

---

imprint [ímprint]   *vt.* 누르다, 찍다

图 mark or stamp with or as if with pressure

图 inscribe, etch, impress, print, stamp

예 *To make a batik, you imprint a design with wax.*

---

treat [tri:t]   *vt.* 대우하다, 다루다

图 interact in a certain way

图 cover, handle, manage, wield, deal with

예 *Treat him with caution, please.*

terrible [térəbl]
a. 무서운

图 causing fear or dread or terror

图 frightful, awful, dreadful, formidable, horrible

예 *a terrible storm*

---

cobble [kábl]
vt. 수선하다

图 repair or mend

图 mend, repair, revamp, patch, sew

예 *The shoes was cobbled.*

---

objection [əbdʒékʃən]
n. 반대

图 the act of protesting

图 opposition, protest, remonstrance, demur, discontent

예 *I feel his objection to going out.*

---

beneficial [benəfiʃəl]
a. 유익한

图 promoting or enhancing well-being

图 gainful, helpful, useful, wholesome, advantageous

예 *The experience was beneficial for her.*

---

replacement [ripléismənt]
n. 교체, 교환

图 the act of furnishing an equivalent person or thing in the place of another

图 change, exchange, substitution, commutation, restoration

예 *Replacement of the star will not be easy.*

---

impeach [impíːtʃ]
vt. 탄핵하다, 비난하다

图 charge with an offense or misdemeanor committed while in office

图 accuse, charge, incriminate, arraign, indict

예 *The President was impeached because of his scandals in 1990s.*

---

survey [sǝrvei]   *vt.* 조사하다

뜻 look over carefully or inspect

동 examine, inspect, research, check, scrutinize

예 *He surveyed his new classmates.*

grief [gríːf]   *n.* 큰 슬픔

뜻 something that causes great unhappiness

동 distress, misery, affliction, sadness, woe

예 *Her death was a great grief to John.*

*Vocabulary/Expressions

vulnerable [vʌlnərəbl]   *a.* 공격받기 쉬운, 상처입기 쉬운
- 医 susceptible to attack
- 동 exposed, susceptible, defenseless, assailable, unsafe
- 예 *a vulnerable bridge*

end [énd]   *vi.* 끝나다
- 医 bring to a conclusion; finish
- 동 conclude, finish, stop, terminate, cease
- 예 *The symphony ends in a pianissimo.*

argue [ɑ́rgjuː]   *vi.* 논하다
- 医 debate of discuss; treat by reasoning
- 동 discuss, contend, debate, quarrel, wrangle
- 예 *He argued with me about this situation.*

local [loukəl]   *a.* 지방의
- 医 relating to or applicable to or concerned with the administration of a city or town or district rather than a larger area
- 동 regional, native, sectional, topical, provincial
- 예 *local taxes*

fume [fjúːm]   *vi.* 연기나다, 그을리다
- 医 emit a cloud of fine particles
- 동 smoke, steam, burn, fumigate, reek
- 예 *The chimney was fuming.*

stiff [stíf]   *a.* 단호한
- 医 marked by firm determination or resolution
- 동 firm, steady, unfaltering, steadfast, unwavering
- 예 *a man of stiff perseverence*

border [bɔ́ːrdər] *vt.* 접경하다
뜻 lie adjacent to another or share a boundary
동 edge, fringe, adjoin, verge, abut
예 *The republic of Korea is bordering the coast.*

---

protection [prətékʃən] *n.* 보호
뜻 the activity of preserving someone or something
동 safeguard, care, security, guardianship, shield
예 *The witnesses demanded police protection.*

---

crisp [krísp] *vt.* 곱슬곱슬하게 하다
뜻 make wrinkles or creases on a smooth surface
동 curl, frizzle, crimp, wave, crinkle
예 *Crisp the paper like this to make a crane.*

---

deadly [dédli] *a.* 치명적인
뜻 causing or capable of causing death
동 killing, deathly, mortal, fatal, murderous
예 *a deadly accident*

---

descendant [diséndənt] *n.* 자손
뜻 a person proceeding from an ancestor
동 offspring, posterity, progeniture, progeny
예 *a direct descendant*

---

neglect [niglékt] *vt.* 무시하다
뜻 give little or no attention to
동 indifferent, disregard, ignore, omit, slight
예 *Neglect the errors.*

affair [əféər]   *n.* 사건, 일

医 a vaguely specified social event

同 business, case, thing, matter, concern

例 *The party was quite an affair.*

---

mechanic [məkǽnik]   *n.* 수리공

医 a craftsman skilled in operating machine tools

同 craftsman, engineer, artisan, machinist, fitter

例 *an automobile motorcar mechanic*

---

grove [gróuv]   *n.* 작은 숲

医 a small growth of trees without underbrush

同 thicket, wood, coppice, spinney, holt

例 *a picnic grove*

---

share [ʃɛ́ər]   *n.* 할당몫, 일부

분医 assets belonging to or due to or contributed by an individual person or group

同 percentage, portaion, part, allotment, division, piece

例 *He wanted his share in cash.*

---

fearful [fíərfəl]   *a.* 무서운

医 causing fear or dread or terror

同 awful, horrible, scary, dreadful, frightful, terrible

例 *the fearful war*

---

assimilate [əsiməleit]   *vi.* 동화되다, 같게 하다, 동질화하다

医 become similar to one's environment

同 conform, homologize, accustom, mingle, accomodate

例 *Immigrants often want to assimilate quickly.*

bail [béil]　　　　　　　　　　　　　　　　　　　　　*n.* 보석금

图 money that must be forfeited by the bondsman if an accused person fails to appear in court for trial

图 security, guarantee, pledge, guaranty, surety

예 *The judge set bail at $10,000.*

---

relief [rilíːf]　　　　　　　　　　　　　　　　　　　*n.* 안도, 안심

图 the feeling that comes when something burdensome is removed or reduced

图 alleviation, comfort, relaxation, softening, consolation

예 *As he heard the news he was suddenly flooded with relief.*

---

emergency [imə́ːrdʒənsi]　　　　　　　　　　　　　*n.* 비상사태

图 a sudden unforeseen crisis that requires immediate action

图 predicament, danger, urgency, crisis, exigency

예 *He never knew what to do in an emergency.*

---

ingredient [ingriːdiənt]　　　　　　　　　　　　　*n.* 요소, 성분

图 an abstract part of something

图 component, element, constituent, factor, part

예 *the grammatical ingredients of a sentence*

---

kin [kín]　　　　　　　　　　　　　　　　　　　　　*n.* 친척

图 group of people related by blood or marriage

图 family, kinship, relative, consanguinity

예 *He's my kin.*

---

bitterly [bitərli]　　　　　　　　　　　　　　　　　*adv.* 격심하게

图 in a resentful manner

图 rancorously, fiercely, keenly, sorely, violently

예 *She complained bitterly.*

acclaim [əkleim]　　　　　　　　　　　　　　　*vt.* 환호하다, 격찬하다

医 praise vociferously

圕 applaud, praise, cheer, admire, compliment, hail, extol

例 *The critics acclaimed the young pianist as a new Rubinstein*

---

relax [rilǽks]　　　　　　　　　　　　　　*vi.* (긴장을) 늦추다, 풀다

医 become less tense, rest, or take one's ease

圕 slacken, loosen, rest, ease, unbend

例 *He relaxed in the hot tub.*

---

segregate [ségrigèit]　　　　　　　　　　　　　　　*vi.* 분리되다

医 divide from the main body or mass and collect

圕 separate, divide, isolate, detach, sequester

例 *Many towns segregated into new counties.*

---

departure [dipá:rtʃər]　　　　　　　　　　　　　　　*n.* 출발

医 act of leaving from somewhere

圕 leaving, deviation, going, starting, takeoff

例 *a neat departure lounge*

---

cruise [krú:z]　　　　　　　　　　　　　　　　*vi.* 순항하다

医 sail or travel about for pleasure, relaxation, or sightseeing

圕 boat, sail, voyage, gallivant, journey

例 *We were cruising in the Caribbean.*

---

balance [bǽləns]　　　　　　　　　　　　　　　　*n.* 균형

医 a state of equilibrium

圕 equilibrium, poise, equipoise, symmetry, equivalence

例 *I lost my balance.*

---

refurbish [riːfə́ːrbiʃ]　　　　　　　　　　*vt.* 다시 닦다, 일신하다
- 医 make brighter and prettier
- 동 renew, freshen up, redo, update, renovate
- 예 *We refurbished the guest wing.*

impede [impiːd]　　　　　　　　　　*vt.* 방해하다
- 医 be a hindrance or obstacle to
- 동 block, inhibit, embarrass, obstruct, prevent
- 예 *She is impeding the progress of our project.*

affect [əfekt]　　　　　　　　　　*vt.* 영향을 미치다
- 医 have an effect upon
- 동 influence, impinge, modify, inspire, transform
- 예 *Will the new rules affect me?*

arbitrary [áːrbətrèri]　　　　　　　　　　*a.* 임의의, 멋대로인
- 医 based on or subject to individual discretion or preference or sometimes impulse or caprice
- 동 tyrannical, autocratic, dictatorial, peremptory, dogmatic
- 예 *an arbitrary decision*

tractable [trǽktəbl]　　　　　　　　　　*a.* 다루기 쉬운
- 医 easily managed (controlled or taught or molded)
- 동 amenable, manageable, docile, pliable, submissive
- 예 *tractable young minds*

immigrant [imigrənt]　　　　　　　　　　*n.* 이주자
- 医 a person who comes to a country where they were not born in order to settle there
- 동 settler, alien, incomer, migrant, emigrant
- 예 *quota immigrant*

18

recreation [rèkriéiʃən]
n. 휴양

医 an activity that diverts or amuses or stimulates

동 diversion, entertainment, refreshment, amusement, pastime

예 *Scuba diving is provided as a recreation for tourists.*

---

detection [ditekʃən]
n. 발견, 탐지

医 the perception that something has occurred or some state exists

동 disclosure, revelation, discovery, finding, sensing

예 *Early detection can often lead to a cure.*

---

indicate [índikèit]
vt. 나타내다

医 be a signal for or a symptom of

동 signify, denote, show, designate, suggest

예 *These symptoms indicate a serious illness.*

---

nutrition [nju:tríʃən]
n. 영양

医 a source of materials to nourish the body

동 diet, alimentation, sustenance, nourishment

예 *He has inadequate nutrition.*

---

coax [kóuks]
vt. 구슬려 시키다

医 influence or urge by gentle urging, caressing, or flattering

동 blandish, flatter, persuade, wheedle, cajole

예 *He coaxed her into going along.*

---

dramatically [drəmǽtikəli]
adv. 극적으로

医 in a very impressive manner

동 effectively, completely, greatly, definitely, excessively

예 *Your performance will improve dramatically.*

deletion [dilíːʃən]   *n.* 삭제

图 the omission that is made when an editorial change shortens a written passage

图 excision, cancellation, erasure, obliteration, effacement

예 *An editor's deletions frequently upset young authors.*

---

brisk [brísk]   *a.* 활발한

图 quick and energetic

图 agile, sprightly, lively, vivacious, spry

예 *a brisk walk in the park*

---

sting [stíŋ]   *vt.* 찌르다

图 cause a sharp or stinging pain or discomfort

图 bite, poke, burn, prick, stab

예 *A bee stung my arm yesterday.*

---

accessible [æksésəbl]   *a.* 접근하기 쉬운

图 capable of being reached

图 exposed, reachable, operative, open, approachable

예 *A town is accessible by rail.*

---

scenery [síːnəri]   *n.* 풍경

图 the appearance of a place

图 view, landscape, spectacle, vista, decor

예 *picturesque scenery*

---

clearance [klíərəns]   *n.* 정리

图 the distance by which one thing clears another

图 removal, chucking, discarding, clearing, dumping

예 *Make a clearance of your desk.*

severe [səvíər]   *a.* 맹렬한

- 図 very strong or vigorous
- 동 strict, harsh, strong, violent, acute
- 예 *severe winds*

---

certification [sə̀:rtəfikéiʃən]   *n.* 증명

- 図 confirmation that some fact or statement is true through the use of documentary evidence
- 동 confirmation, attestation, corroboration, testimonial, certificate
- 예 *certification of teachers*

---

enthusiastic [inθuːziǽstik]   *a.* 열렬한

图 having or showing great excitement and interest

통 excited, eager, keen, zealous, ardent

예 *Enthusiastic crowds filled the streets.*

---

fine [fàin]   *a.* 훌륭한

图 characterized by elegance or refinement or accomplishment

통 delicate, good, nice, pretty, excellent

예 *a fine gentleman*

---

stick [stík]   *vt.* 찌르다

图 put, fix, force, or implant

통 insert, pierce, impale, thrust, penetrate

예 *Stick your thumb in the crack.*

---

untapped [ʌntǽpt]   *a.* 이용되지 않은

图 not drawn upon or used

통 natural, fresh, untouched, unused, immaculate

예 *untapped reserves of coal*

---

contagious [kəntéidʒəs]   *a.* 전염성의

图 capable of being transmitted by infection

통 catching, infectious, communicable, pestiferous, taking, spreading

예 *a contagious disease*

---

repulsive [ripʌlsiv]   *a.* 불쾌한

图 offensive to the mind

통 hideous, abhorrent, obscene, repugnant, detestable

예 *repulsive behavior*

---

wrap [ræp]   *vt.* 싸다

医 arrange or fold as a cover or protection

통 cover, pack, muffle, envelop, swathe

예 *Wrap the present.*

---

culprit [kʌlprit]   *n.* 범죄자

医 someone who perpetrates wrongdoing

통 defendant, criminal, malefactor, perpetrator, offender

예 *He avowed him to be the culprit of the case.*

---

union [juːnjən]   *n.* 결합, 연합

医 the state of being joined or united or linked

통 alliance, coalition, unification, federation, association

예 *There is strength in union.*

---

durable [djúərəbl]   *a.* 영속성 있는

医 existing for a long time

통 permanent, abiding, lasting, enduring, stable

예 *I hope for a durable peace.*

---

proclamation [pràkləméiʃən]   *n.* 선언

医 a formal public statement

통 manifesto, declaration, promulgation, announcement, statement

예 *a proclamation of independence*

---

exclusion [iksklúːʒən]   *n.* 제외

医 the act of forcing out someone or something

통 elimination, preclusion, exception, riddance, expulsion

예 *the child's exclusion from school*

---

vacuum [vǽkjuəm]

n. 빈곳

- 图 an empty area or space
- 图 vacancy, blank, emptiness, void
- 예 *the vacuum of outer space*

insurance [inʃúərəns]

n. 보험

- 图 promise of reimbursement in the case of loss
- 图 assurance, guarantee, indemnity, coverage, safeguard
- 예 *You should have read the small print on your insurance.*

represent [reprizent]

vt. 나타내다

- 图 express indirectly by an image, form, or model
- 图 depict, picture, describe, portray, show
- 예 *What does the Statue of Liberty represent?*

truth [trúːθ]

n. 진실

- 图 conformity to reality or actuality
- 图 reality, veracity, sooth, verity, fidelity
- 예 *They debated the truth of the proposition.*

donation [dounéiʃən]

n. 기부

- 图 act of giving in common with others for a common purpose especially to a charity
- 图 contribution, grant, endowment, offering, presentation
- 예 *a voluntary donation*

duty [djúːti]

n. 의무

- 图 the social force that binds you to the courses of action demanded by that force
- 图 responsibility, assignment, obligation, function, undertaking
- 예 *We must instill a sense of duty in our children.*

utilize [júːtəlàiz] 　　　　　　　　　　　　　　　　*vt.* 이용하다

㊟ put into service

㊟ make use of, apply, take advantage of, use, employ

㊟ *How do you utilize this tool?*

---

inexpensive [ìnikspénsiv] 　　　　　　*a.* 비용이 많이 들지 않는

㊟ relatively low in price or charging low prices

㊟ cheap, modest, economical, thrifty, reasonable

㊟ *inexpensive family restaurants*

---

arrest [ərést] 　　　　　　　　　　　　　　　　　*vt.* 체포하다

㊟ take into custody

㊟ seize, capture, detain, apprehend, nab

㊟ *The police arrested the suspected criminals.*

---

profess [prəfés] 　　　　　　　　　　*vt.* 공언하다, 고백하다

㊟ confess one's faith in, or allegiance to

㊟ assert, declare, confess, proclaim, confirm

㊟ *The terrorists professed allegiance to their country.*

---

decent [díːsnt] 　　　　　　　　　　　　　　　　　*a.* 점잖은

㊟ according with custom or propriety

㊟ decorous, proper, modest, seemly, respectable

㊟ *decent behavior*

---

dilute [dailuːt] 　　　　　　　　　　　　　　　*vt.* 묽게 하다

㊟ lessen the strength or flavor of a solution or mixture

㊟ deliquesce, adulterate, rarefy, attenuate, weaken

㊟ *She dilutes milk with water.*

journal [dʒə́:rnl]
n. 신문, 잡지

图 a periodical dedicated to a particular subject

图 newspaper, magazine, periodical, review, paper

예 *He reads the medical journals.*

reckon [rékən]
vt. 생각하다

图 expect, believe, or suppose

图 think, guess, suppose, imagine, opine

예 *He didn't reckon to find her in the kitchen.*

wet [wét]
a. 젖은

图 covered or soaked with a liquid such as water

图 damp, moist, watery, humid, soggy

예 *a wet bathing suit*

violate [vaiəleit]
vt. 위반하다

图 act in disregard of laws, rules, contracts, or promises

图 infringe, breach, offend, infract, transgress

예 *He violated the basic laws of human civilization.*

adapt [ədǽpt]
vi. 적응하다

图 conform oneself to new or different conditions

图 conform, adjust, fit, accommodate, suit

예 *We must adapt to the bad economic situation.*

evidence [evədəns]
n. 증거

图 knowledge on which to base belief

图 corroboration, indication, clue, proof, attestation

예 *The evidence that smoking causes lung cancer is very compelling.*

dividend [dívədend] *n.* 배당금, 분배금

뜻 that part of the earnings of a corporation that is distributed to its shareholders.

동 bonus, allotment, meed

예 *bonus dividend*

---

scramble [skrǽmbl] *vi.* 기어오르다

뜻 climb awkwardly, as if by scrambling

동 struggle, trek, clamber, shin, climb

예 *The friend scrambled after them.*

---

libel [làibəl] *vt.* 중상하다, 비방하다

뜻 print slanderous statements against

동 asperse, bad-mouth, defame, burlesque, denigrate

예 *The newspaper was accused of libeling him.*

---

property [prápərti] *n.* 재산, 소유물

뜻 something owned

동 estate, possessions, wealth, holding, belongings

예 *That hat is my property.*

---

gulp [gʌlp] *vi.* 꿀꺽꿀꺽 마시다

뜻 swallow hurriedly or greedily or in one draught

동 devour, quaff, swig, imbibe, wolf

예 *The men gulped down their beers.*

---

attribute [ətríbjuːt] *vt.* ~의 탓으로 하다

뜻 credit to; consider as due or appropriate to

동 assign, impute, accredit, refer, ascribe

예 *She attributed her success to unwavering intergrity.*

---

transact [trænsǽkt]
vi. 거래하다

图 conduct business

图 conduct, accomplish, operate, perform, execute

예 *The man illegally transacted with foreign governments.*

proof [prú:f]
n. 증명, 증거

图 any factual evidence that helps to establish the truth of something

图 evidence, authentication, demonstration, confirmation, testimony

예 *If you have any proof for what you say, now is the time to produce it.*

revise [rivaiz]
vt. 교정하다

图 reorganize, especially for the purpose of updating and improving

图 alter, review, correct, amend, modify

예 *He revised his thesis.*

trip [tríp]
n. 여행

图 a journey for some purpose

图 journey, excursion, tour, voyage, travel

예 *He took a trip to the shopping center.*

collision [kəlíʒən]
n. 충돌, 격돌

图 an accident resulting from violent impact of a moving object

图 conflict, smash, crash, encounter, impact

예 *Three passengers were killed in the collision.*

allow [əlau]
vt. 허락하다

图 consent to, give permission

图 accept, concede, let, admit, permit

예 *I cannot allow you to see your exam.*

adversity [ædvə́:rsəti]　　　　　　　　　　　*n.* 불운

图 a state of misfortune or affliction

图 suffering, hardship, distress, misfortune, torment

예 *a life of adversity*

---

assiduous [əsídʒuəs]　　　　　　　　　　*a.* 근면한

图 marked by care and persistent effort

图 diligent, painstaking, hard-working, sedulous, industrious

예 *She has assiduous attempts to learn French.*

---

novelty [návəlti]　　　　　　　　　　　*n.* 진기함

图 originality by virtue of being new and surprising

图 originality, innovation, newness, recency

예 *a novelty shop*

---

decay [dikéi]　　　　　　　　　　　*vi.* 부식하다, 썩다

图 fall into ruin

图 decline, molder, decompose, rot, putrefy

예 *The unoccupied house started to decay.*

---

supervisor [su:pərvaizər]　　　　　　　　*n.* 감독자

图 one who oversees or has charge and direction of

图 overseer, controller, superintendent, inspector, manager

예 *night supervisor*

---

cutback [kʌtbæk]　　　　　　　　　　　*n.* 삭감

图 a reduction in quantity or rate

图 curtailment, diminution, reduction, decrement, abatement

예 *cutback in production*

monarch [mánərk]

n. 군주

图 a nation's ruler or head of state usually by hereditary right

동 king, prince, ruler, sovereign, potentate

예 *an absolute monarch*

adjust [ədʒʌst]

vt. 조절하다

图 alter or regulate so as to achieve accuracy or conform to a standard

동 settle, correct, set, tune, fit

예 *Adjust the clock, please.*

*Vocabulary/Expressions

scale [skeil]　　　　　　　　　　　　　　　　　　　*n.* 규모
- 英 an ordered reference standard
- 동 spread, hierarchy, scope, measure, size
- 예 *They hold a meeting on a large scale.*

---

loan [loun]　　　　　　　　　　　　　　　　　　　*n.* 대부
- 英 the temporary provision of money
- 동 debt, advance, borrowing, accommodation, mortgage
- 예 *bank loan*

---

district [dístrikt]　　　　　　　　　　　　　　　*n.* 지역, 구역
- 英 a region marked off for administrative or other purposes
- 동 zone, region, section, area, province
- 예 *business district*

---

grasp [grǽsp]　　　　　　　　　　　　　　　　　*vt.* 움켜잡다
- 英 hold firmly
- 동 grab, clutch, apprehend, gripe, seize
- 예 *I grasp a handrail.*

---

detain [ditéin]　　　　　　　　　　　　　　*vt.* 못가게 붙들다
- 英 cause to be slowed down or delayed
- 동 arrest, hold, restrain, delay, withhold
- 예 *Traffic was detained by the bad weather.*

---

freight [freit]　　　　　　　　　　　　　　　　　*n.* 화물
- 英 goods carried by a large vehicle
- 동 cargo, load, shipment, consignment, lading
- 예 *freight car*

---

resource [ri:sɔ:rs]   *n.* 자원

圏 a source of aid or support that may be drawn upon when needed

동 reserve, property, reservoir, store, assets

예 *The local library is a valuable resource.*

appeal [əpí:l]   *vi.* 호소하다

圏 ask for aid or protection

동 plead, solicit, crave, invoke, beseech

예 *He appealed to me for help.*

execute [eksikju:t]   *vt.* 실행하다

圏 carry out or perform an action

동 do, fulfil, perform, accomplish, realize

예 *The skater executed a triple pirouette.*

withdraw [wiðdrɔ:]   *vi.* 물러나다

圏 pull back or move away or backward

동 retire, recall, retract, recede, retreat

예 *The enemy withdrew.*

deal [di:l]   *vt.* 다루다

圏 take into consideration for exemplifying purposes

동 take, handle, consider, sell, treat

예 *Deal the following case.*

disapprove [dìsəprú:v]   *vi.* 찬성하지 않다

圏 deem wrong or inappropriate

동 discountenance, reject, deprecate, reprobate, disfavor

예 *I disapprove of her child rearing methods.*

plaintiff [pléintif]   *n.* 원고

医 a person who brings an action in a court of law

동 prosecutor, complainant, accuser, petitioner, suer

예 *a plaintiff's lawyer*

---

embezzle [imbezl]   *vt.* 횡령하다

医 appropriate fraudulently to one's own use

동 misappropriate, usurp, defalcate, abstract, malversate, peculate

예 *The accountant embezzled thousands of dollars while working for the wealthy family.*

---

gust [gʌst]   *n.* 질풍

医 a strong current of air

동 blast, flurry, blow, tempest, squall

예 *The tree was bent almost double by the gust.*

---

pertinent [pə́:rtənənt]   *a.* 적절한

医 being of striking appropriateness

동 appropriate, proper, aptelevant, suitable

예 *a pertinent reply*

---

chance [tʃǽns]   *a.* 우연한

医 occurring or appearing or singled out by chance

동 accidental, casual, contingent, coincidental, fortuitous

예 *a chance occurrence*

---

enhancement [inhǽnsmənt]   *n.* 상승, 향상

医 an improvement that makes something more agreeable

동 improvement, rise, increase, development, enrichment, augmentation

예 *revenue enhancement*

---

optimistic [àptəmístik] *a.* 낙천적인

圏 expecting the best in this best of all possible worlds

동 positive, hopeful, affirmative, sanguine, upbeat

예 *optimistic plans*

---

stumble [stʌmbl] *vi.* 비틀거리며 걷다

圏 walk unsteadily

동 stagger, falter, slip, trip, bumble

예 *The drunk man stumbled about.*

---

considerable [kənsídərəbl] *a.* 상당한

圏 large or relatively large in number or amount or extent or degree

동 substantial, sizable, important, significant, notable

예 *He spent a considerable amount of time on the problem.*

---

control [kəntróul] *vt.* 지배하다

圏 exercise authoritative power over

동 manage, govern, direct, rule, supervise

예 *The officer controls the military forces.*

---

revitalize [ri:vaitəlaiz] *vt.* 생기를 회복시키다

圏 restore strength

동 refresh, exhilarate, regenerate, enliven

예 *This food revitalized the patient.*

---

inherit [inhérit] *vt.* 물려받다

圏 receive from a predecessor

동 take over, derive, granted, succeed, receive

예 *The new chairman inherited many problems from the previous chair.*

garment [gɑ́ːrmənt]
n. 의복

- 图 an article of clothing
- 图 clothes, apparel, dress, raiment, garb
- 예 *garments of the finest silk*

---

coalition [kouəliʃən]
n. 연합

- 图 the union of diverse things into one body or form or group
- 图 combination, association, fusion, union, bloc
- 예 *He breaked up a coalition.*

---

excerpt [éksəːrpt]
vi. 발췌하다, 인용하다

- 图 take out of a literary work in order to cite or copy
- 图 quote, extract, select, cite, pick
- 예 *This is the small excerpt from the famous novel "The Last Lecture".*

---

aggravate [ǽgrəveit]
vt. 악화시키다

- 图 make worse
- 图 worsen, vex, complicate, intensify, exacerbate
- 예 *This drug aggravates the pain.*

---

portfolio [pɔːrtfouliou]
n. 서류첩

- 图 a large, flat, thin case for carrying loose papers or drawings or maps
- 图 brief bag, briefcase, envelope, folder, container
- 예 *He remembered her because she was carrying a large portfolio.*

---

depreciation [diprìːʃiéiʃən]
n. 가치 하락

- 图 a decrease in price or value
- 图 devaluation, fall, deflation, reduction, slump
- 예 *depreciation of the dollar against the yen*

---

certificate [sərtifikət]

n. 증명서

图 a document attesting to the truth of certain stated facts

图 diploma, credentials, testimonial, affirmation, endorsement

에 *He has several valuable certificates.*

---

solicit [səlísit]

vt. 간청하다

图 make an entreaty for something

图 implore, petition, ask, beg, request

에 *My neighbor keeps soliciting money for different charities.*

---

clothes [klóuz]

n. 옷

图 covering for the human body

图 dress, apparel, garb, clothing, raiment

에 *He always bought his clothes at the same store.*

---

isolation [àisəléiʃən]

n. 격리

图 a state of separation between persons or groups

图 segregation, separation, solitude, insulation, seclusion

에 *social isolation*

---

depend [dipénd]

vi. 의존하다

图 have faith or confidence in

图 hope, lean, count, entrust, rely

에 *You have to depend on your family in times of crisis.*

---

investigation [invèstəgéiʃən]

n. 조사, 연구

图 an inquiry into unfamiliar or questionable activities

图 inquest, examination, inquiry, research, study

에 *There was a congressional investigation into the scandal.*

---

transgress [trænsgrés]   *vt.* 위반하다

图 act in disregard of laws, rules, contracts, or promises

图 violate, offend, contravene, breach, infract

예 *I transgressed the speed regulations.*

---

howl [hàul]   *vi.* 울부짖다

图 emit long loud cries

图 roar, wail, yaup, ululate, yawl

예 *She is howling with sorrow.*

---

insufferable [insʌfərəbl]   *a.* 비위에 거슬리는, 밉상스러운

图 used of persons or their behavior

图 unendurable, intolerable, impossible, unbearable, insupportable

예 *insufferable behavior*

---

stabilize [stéibəlàiz]   *vt.* 안정시키다

图 make keep from fluctuating or put into an equilibrium

图 steady, firm, balance, preserve, settle

예 *The drug stabilized her blood pressure.*

---

vomit [vámit]   *vi.* 토하다

图 eject the contents of the stomach through the mouth

图 throw up, disgorge, spue, puke, spew

예 *After drinking too much, the students vomited.*

---

automatic [ɔːtəmǽtik]   *a.* 자동의

图 operating with minimal human intervention

图 self-regulating, reflex, perfunctory, self-acting, mechanical

예 *automatic transmission*

---

reckless [réklis]　　　　　　　　　　　　　　　　　　　　*a.* 무모한

뜻 marked by defiant disregard for danger or consequences

동 foolhardy, heedless, imprudent, rash, heady

예 *a reckless driver*

---

inoculate [inákjulèit]　　　　　　　　　　　　　　　　　*vi.* 접종하다

뜻 perform vaccinations or produce immunity in by inoculation

동 immunize, vaccinate, graft, engraft

예 *We inoculate against scarlet fever.*

---

corruption [kərʌpʃən]　　　　　　　　　　　　　　　　　*n.* 타락, 퇴폐

뜻 impairment of virtue and moral principles

동 venality, bribery, degeneracy, putrefaction, depravity

예 *Rome had fallen into moral corruption.*

---

surprise [sərpràiz]　　　　　　　　　　　　　　　　　　*vt.* 놀라게 하다

뜻 strike with wonder and astonishment by something sudden, unexpected

동 astound, amaze, startle, astonish, disconcert

예 *The news really surprised me.*

---

enchant [intʃǽnt]　　　　　　　　　　　　　　　　　　*vt.* 매혹하다

뜻 cause to be enamored

동 charm, fascinate, attract, spellbind, enthral

예 *She enchanted all the men's hearts.*

---

subsequent [sʌbsikwənt]　　　　　　　　　　　　　　　*a.* 다음의

뜻 following in time or order

동 successive, following, next, ensuing, posterior

예 *subsequent developments*

dictator [dikteitər]　　　　　　　　　　　　　　　　　*n.* 독재자, 절대 권력자

㊁ a ruler who is unconstrained by law

㊂ despot, authoritarian, potentate, absolutist, tyrant

㊀ *a cruel dictator*

---

fixed [fikst]　　　　　　　　　　　　　　　　　　　　*a.* 고정된

㊁ made firm, fastened immovably

㊂ firm, stationary, rigid, set, immovable

㊀ *The policy is fixed.*

---

*Vocabulary/Expressions

---

premise [premis]   *n.* 전제

图 a statement that is assumed to be true and from which a conclusion can be drawn

동 assumption, supposition, prerequisite, thesis

예 *On the premise that he has been injured we can infer that he will not to play.*

---

invisible [invízəbl]   *a.* 눈에 안 보이는

图 impossible or nearly impossible to see

동 unseen, imperceptible, sightless, concealed, viewless

예 *an invisible hinge*

---

shopper [ʃápər]   *n.* 물건 사는 사람

图 someone who visits stores in search of articles to buy

동 client, buyer, customer, purchaser, consumer

예 *a window shopper*

---

prescribe [priskraib]   *vt.* 규정하다, 명령하다, 지시하다

图 issue commands or orders for

동 command, order, direct, guide, rule

예 *He prescribed the children to do their homework.*

---

alienate [éiljənèit]   *vt.* 소원하게 하다, 이간하다

图 arouse hostility or indifference in where there had formerly been love, affection, or friendliness

동 separate, disunite, estrange, turn away, disaffect

예 *She alienated her friends when she became fanatically religious.*

---

association [əsousieiʃən]
n. 단체

医 a formal organization of people or groups of people

통 corporation, society, union, guild, organization

예 *He joined the Modern Language Association.*

available [əvéiləbl]
a. 이용할 수 있는

医 obtainable or accessible and ready for use or service

통 disposable, applicable, obtainable, accessible, serviceable

예 *This medicine is available over the counter.*

intervene [ìntərvíːn]
vi. 간섭하다, 개입하다

医 get involved, so as to alter or hinder an action, or through force or threat of force

통 interfere, intercede, meddle, step in, interpose

예 *Why did the U.S. not intervene earlier in WW II?*

oppress [əprés]
vt. 압박하다

医 come down on or keep down by unjust use of one's authority

통 suppress, depress, crush, persecute, tyrannize

예 *The government oppresses political activists.*

headquarters [hedkwɔ:rtərz]
n. 본부

医 the office that serves as the administrative center of an enterprise

통 home office, head office, central office, home base, main office

예 *Many companies have their headquarters in New York.*

accrue [əkru:]
vi. (이익 등이) 생기다, (이자가) 붙다

医 grow by addition

통 build up, accumulate, gather, increase, amass

예 *The interest accrues.*

foggy [fɔ:gi]　　　　　　　　　　　　　　　　　　*a.* 안개가 자욱한

图 filled or abounding with fog or mist

동 misty, cloudy, hazy, brumous, nebulous

예 *a foggy October morning*

---

rebate [rí:beit]　　　　　　　　　　　　　　　　　*n.* 환불

图 a refund of some fraction of the amount paid

동 deduction, abatement, discount, reduction, allowance

예 *a tax rebate*

---

condense [kəndens]　　　　　　　　　　　　　　　*vt.* 요약하다

图 make more concise

동 abbreviate, compress, epitomize, summate, concentrate

예 *Condense the contents of a book into a summary.*

---

initial [iniʃəl]　　　　　　　　　　　　　　　　　*a.* 처음의, 최초의

图 occurring at the beginning

동 first, inceptive, original, primary, incipient

예 *I took the initial step toward reconciliation.*

---

circulation [sə̀:rkjuleiʃən]　　　　　　　　　*n.* 유통, 유포, 전달

图 the spread or transmission of something (as news or money) to a wider group or area

동 distribution, spread, apportionment, transmission, dissemination, currency

예 *currency circulation*

---

cherish [tʃériʃ]　　　　　　　　　　　　　　　　*vt.* 소중히 하다

图 be fond of

동 glorify, adore, esteem, respect, commend

예 *He cherishes a friendship.*

---

certified [sə́:rtəfàid]
a. 보증된

图 holding appropriate documentation and officially on record as qualified to perform a specified function or practice a specified skill

图 authorized, registered, confirmed, qualified, vouched for

예 *a certified hospital*

disconsolate [diskánsələt]
a. 우울한

图 causing dejection

图 sad, gloomy, comfortless, desolate, inconsolable

예 *a disconsolate winter landscape*

opposite [ápəzit]
a. 반대편의

图 being directly across from each other

图 adverse, converse, opposed, contrary, reverse

예 *opposite meanings*

separate [sépərèit]
vt. 가르다

图 divide into parts or portions

图 segregate, part, divide, split, dissever

예 *He separated the fighting children.*

scrap [skrǽp]
n. 한 조각, 파편, 단편

图 a small fragment of something broken off from the whole

图 chip, piece, fragment, shred, bit

예 *A scrap of rock caught him in the eye.*

cautious [kɔ́:ʃəs]
a. 신중한

图 showing careful forethought

图 careful, prudent, chary, circumspect, wary

예 *cautious guarded optimism*

bring [bríŋ] *vt.* 가져오다

뜻 take something or somebody with oneself somewhere

동 carry, get, fetch, take, convey

예 *Bring me the box from the other room.*

---

amendment [əméndmənt] *n.* 개정, 수정

뜻 an alternation or change for better

동 alteration, modification, correction, emendation, rectification

예 *He must adopt this amendment.*

---

indict [indait] *vt.* 고발하다

뜻 accuse formally of a crime

동 impeach, accuse, charge, incriminate, prosecute

예 *I indicted him as a murderer.*

---

clear [klíər] *a.* 명백한

뜻 the state of being free of suspicion

동 lucid, perspicuous, distinct, pellucid, transparent

예 *Investigation showed that he was in the clear.*

---

duplicate [djú:plikət] *n.* 복제

뜻 copy that corresponds to an original exactly

동 reproduction, copy, duplication, replica, transcription

예 *He made a duplicate for the files.*

---

pharmacist [fá:rməsist] *n.* 약사

뜻 a health professional trained in the art of preparing and dispensing drugs

동 druggist, chemist, dispenser, apothecary

예 *A pharmacist is not qualified to provide medicine.*

slip [slip] vi. 미끄러지다

뜻 move obliquely or sideways, usually in an uncontrolled manner

동 slide, glide, skid, move, slither

예 *The wheels slipped against the sidewalk.*

custody [kʌstədi] n. 보관, 관리

뜻 care, watch, inspection for keeping, preservation or security

동 conservation, protection, hands, supervision

예 *Your guests are now in my custody.*

denomination [dinàmənéiʃən] n. 명명, 명칭

뜻 identifying word or words by which someone or something is called and classified or distinguished from others

동 designation, name, appellation, title, sect

예 *The NGO changed their denomination.*

quit [kwit] vt. 그만두다

뜻 put an end to a state or an activity

동 give up, cease, stop, discontinue, leave

예 *Quit teasing your little brother.*

forfeit [fɔːrfit] n. 벌금, 과료, 추징금

뜻 a penalty for a fault or mistake that involves losing or giving up something

동 compensation, fine, penalty, amends, reparation

예 *The contract specified forfeits if the work was not completed on time.*

diverge [divə́ːrdʒ] vt. 분기하다, 갈라지다

뜻 extend in a different direction

동 digress, separate, deviate, vary, differ

예 *The lines start to diverge here.*

circulate [sə́:rkjulèit]   *vt.* (소문을) 퍼뜨리다

- 医 cause to become widely known
- 동 distribute, broadcast, propagate, disseminate, spread
- 예 *He circulates the information.*

mash [mæʃ]   *vt.* 짓찧다

- 医 compress with violence, out of natural shape or condition
- 동 smash, squash, crush, squeeze, squelch
- 예 *Mash an aluminum can.*

project [prádʒekt]   *n.* 계획, 기획

- 医 any piece of work that is undertaken or attempted
- 동 scheme, blueprint, plan, idea, task
- 예 *He prepared for great projects.*

fraud [frɔːd]   *n.* 사기

- 医 something intended to deceive
- 동 deceit, fake, cheat, swindle
- 예 *He was accused of fraud.*

apply [əplai]   *vt.* 적용하다

- 医 put into service
- 동 use, assign, practice, employ, utilize
- 예 *I apply this rule to get good results.*

expect [ikspékt]   *vt.* 기대하다, 예상하다

- 医 regard something as probable or likely
- 동 anticipate, await, reckon, suppose, surmise
- 예 *The meteorologists are expecting rain for tomorrow.*

equivocal [ikwívəkəl]　　　　　　　　　　　　　　*a.* 모호한

图 open to two or more interpretations

图 ambiguous, doubtful, suspicious, uncertain, dubious

예 *an equivocal statement*

---

computation [kàmpjutéi∫ən]　　　　　　　　　*n.* 계산

图 the procedure of calculating

图 estimate, calculation, numeration, account, reckoning

예 *an approximate computation*

---

registration [redʒistrei∫ən]　　　　　　　　*n.* 등록, 기재

图 the act of enrolling

图 entry, listing, recording, enrollment, registry

예 *resident registration*

---

evacuate [ivǽkjueit]　　　　　　　　　　　　*vt.* 피난시키다

图 move out of an unsafe location into safety

图 displace, escape, abandon, vamoose, depart

예 *After the earthquake, residents were evacuated.*

---

career [kəriər]　　　　　　　　　　　　　　*n.* 경력

图 the general progression of your working or professional life

图 course, record, personal history, life history, antecedent

예 *The general had had a distinguished career.*

---

probe [próub]　　　　　　　　　　　　　　*vt.* 규명하다

图 question or examine thoroughly and closely

图 sound, explore, scrutinize, investigate, search

예 *He probed the scandals in 1800s.*

personnel [pə̀:rsənel]   *n.* 직원

图 group of people willing to obey orders

图 faculty, staff, employee, members, workers

예 *A public personnel is necessary to give security to the rights of citizens.*

---

expensive [ikspénsiv]   *a.* 값비싼

图 high in price or charging high prices

图 costly, valuable, precious, dear, sumptuous

예 *expensive clothes*

---

receive [risi:v]   *vt.* 받다

图 come into possession of

图 derive, catch, gain, inherit, accept

예 *I received letters from the front.*

---

*Vocabulary/Expressions

Day 6

assist [əsist]   *vt.* 돕다
- 医 give support to in some undertaking or effort
- 同 support, aid, help, befriend, collaborate
- 예 *Can you assist me carry this table?*

luxurious [lʌgʒuəriəs]   *a.* 사치스러운
- 医 displaying luxury and furnishing gratification to the senses
- 同 deluxe, lavish, affluent, indulgent, elaborate, opulent
- 예 *a luxurious banquet*

depressed [diprést]   *a.* 의기소침한
- 医 filled with melancholy and despondency
- 同 sad, dejected, dispirited, gloomy, despondent
- 예 *He is depressed by the loss of his job.*

excavate [ékskəvèit]   *vt.* (구멍을) 파다
- 医 remove the inner part or the core of
- 同 grub, dig, scoop, unearth, delve
- 예 *The mining company wants to excavate the hillside.*

distribution [dìstrəbjúːʃən]   *n.* 분배
- 医 the spatial or geographic property of being scattered about over a range, area, or volume
- 同 division, allocation, dispensation, apportionment, partition
- 예 *After the revolution, food distribution was decentralized.*

forecast [fɔːrkæ̀st]   *vt.* 예보하다
- 医 predict in advance
- 同 predict, anticipate, presage, foretell, prognosticate
- 예 *The caster forecasts the weather in the morning.*

aptitude [ǽptətjuːd]

n. 재능

图 inherent ability

图 ability, faculty, capability, gift, talent

예 *She has an aptitude for playing the piano.*

foundation [faundeiʃən]

n. 토대

图 the basis on which something is grounded

图 basis, groundwork, establishment, infrastructure, root

예 *There is little foundation for his objections.*

confiscate [kánfəskeit]

vt. 몰수하다

图 take temporary possession of as a security, by legal authority

图 seize, expropriate, accroach, impound, sequester

예 *The FBI confiscated the drugs.*

spare [spéər]

a. 여분의

图 more than is needed, desired, or required

图 excess, redundant, extra, surplus, supererogatory

예 *I found some spare change lying on the dresser.*

council [kàunsəl]

n. 회의

图 a meeting of people for consultation

图 gathering, assembly, conference, convention

예 *I have an emergency council now.*

press [prés]

vi. 내리누르다

图 exert pressure or force to or upon

图 push, squeeze, crush, iron, jam

예 *He pressed down on the boards.*

deteriorate [ditiəriəreit] *vi.* 나빠지다

㈜ grow worse

㈜ debase, impair, spoil, worsen, degenerate

㈜ *Her condition deteriorated.*

---

indomitable [indάmətəbl] *a.* 굴복하지 않는

㈜ impossible to subdue

㈜ steadfast, invincible, tameless, impregnable, unyielding

㈜ *an indomitable spirit*

---

marital [mǽrətl] *a.* 결혼의, 부부의

㈜ of or relating to the state of marriage

㈜ married, conjugal, nuptial, wedded, hymeneal

㈜ *marital status*

---

natural [nǽtʃərəl] *a.* 타고난

㈜ being talented through inherited qualities

㈜ inborn, native, innate, unaffected, inbred

㈜ *a natural leader*

---

fee [fíː] *n.* 보수, 요금

㈜ a fixed charge for a privilege or for professional services

㈜ charge, pay, cost, payment, honorarium

㈜ *tuition fees*

---

actually [ǽktʃuəli] *adv.* 실제로

㈜ in actual fact

㈜ practically, really, indeed, in fact, truly

㈜ *No one actually saw the shark.*

comfortable [kʌmftəbl]   *a.* 편안한

图 free from stress or conducive to mental ease

图 cozy, agreeable, easy, comfy, snug

예 *She's a comfortable person to be with.*

---

reprimand [réprəmænd]   *vt.* 꾸짖다

图 censure severely or angrily

图 rebuke, scold, objurgate, admonish, upbraid

예 *The deputy reprimanded the Prime Minister.*

---

commute [kəmjúːt]   *vi.* 교환하다

图 exchange positions without a change in value

图 transpose, change, switch, exchange, trade

예 *These operators commute with each other.*

---

executive [igzekjutiv]   *n.* 임원

图 a person responsible for the administration of a business

图 director, administrator, manager, chief, officer

예 *a business executive*

---

hospitable [háspitəbl]   *a.* 친절한

图 disposed to treat guests and strangers with cordiality and generosity

图 friendly, kind, generous, considerate, obliging

예 *a hospitable act*

---

affluent [æfluənt]   *a.* 풍족한

图 having an abundant supply of money or possessions of value

图 abundant, moneyed, copious, wealthy, opulent

예 *an affluent banker*

---

double [dʌbl] *a.* 2배의, 이중의

医 having more than one decidedly dissimilar aspects or qualities

동 dual, binal, diploid, twofold, bifold

예 *a double lock*

---

indoors [indɔ́ːrz] *a.* 실내에서

医 within a building

동 inside, under a roof, interior, inwardly, within

예 *In winter, we usually play indoors.*

---

additive [ǽdətiv] *a.* 부가적인

医 characterized or produced by addition

동 extra, additional, incremental, cumulative, summative

예 *an additive process*

---

criminal [krímənl] *n.* 범죄자

医 someone who has committed a crime or has been legally convicted of a crime

동 offender, felon, malefactor, perpetrator, culprit

예 *a habitual criminal*

---

withstand [wiθstǽnd] *vt.* 저항하다

医 resist or confront with resistance

동 bear, oppose, endure, hold out, resist

예 *The new material withstands even the greatest wear and tear.*

---

confrontation [kànfrəntéiʃən] *n.* 대면, 대결

医 the act of hostile groups opposing each other

동 encounter, affray, dispute, contest, opposition, strife

예 *The government was not ready for a confrontation with the unions.*

intimidate [intímədèit]   *vt.* 겁주다, 협박하다

뜻 make timid or fearful

동 scare, appal, frighten, threaten, daunt

예 *Her boss is intimidating her by a phonecall.*

---

navigate [nǽvəgèit]   *vi.* 항해하다

뜻 travel on water propelled by wind or by other means

동 journey, cruise, sail, voyage, steer

예 *The QE2 will navigate to Southampton tomorrow.*

---

robust [roubʌst]   *a.* 강건한

뜻 sturdy and strong in form, constitution, or construction

동 burly, sturdy, healthy, stalwart, powerful

예 *a robust body*

---

dwindle [dwíndl]   *vi.* 점차 감소하다

뜻 become smaller or lose substance

동 decrease, lessen, diminish, shrink, wane, abate

예 *Her savings dwindled down.*

---

stimulation [stìmjuléiʃən]   *n.* 자극

뜻 the act of arousing an organism to action

동 provocation, excitation, incitement, encouragement, stimulus

예 *ellectual stimulation*

---

cancel [kǽnsəl]   *vt.* 취소하다

뜻 postpone indefinitely or annul something that was scheduled

동 nullify, rescind, undo, countermand, revoke

예 *We canceled the dinner party.*

appraisal [əpreizəl]   *n.* 견적, 평가

图 the classification of someone or something with respect to its worth

图 estimate, assessment, evaluation, rating, reckoning

예 *performance appraisal*

---

blaze [bléiz]   *vi.* 타오르다

图 shine brightly and intensively

图 burn, flame, glow, shine, flare

예 *Meteors blazed across the atmosphere.*

---

hoarse [hɔːrs]   *a.* 쉰 목소리의

图 deep and harsh sounding as if from shouting or illness or emotion

图 rough, husky, raucous, gruff, throaty

예 *hoarse cries*

---

commercial [kəmə́ːrʃəl]   *a.* 상업상의

图 connected with or engaged in or sponsored by or used in commerce or
commercial enterprises

图 marketable, financial, fiscal, monetary, economic

예 *commercial trucker*

---

infringe [infrindʒ]   *vt.* 위반하다

图 go against, as of rules and laws

图 contravene, transgress, violate, trespass, invade

예 *He infringed a law.*

---

industrial [indʌstriəl]   *a.* 산업의

图 of or relating to or resulting from industry

图 industrialized, commercial, manufacturing, business, technical

예 *industrial output*

optional [ápʃənl]   *a.* 선택의

图 possible but not necessary

图 alternative, voluntary, discretional, noncompulsory, facultative

예 *an optional subject*

---

inhabitation [inhæbətéiʃən]   *n.* 주거

图 the act of dwelling in or living permanently in a place

图 house, dwelling, residence, abode

예 *He studied the creation and inhabitation and demise of the colony.*

---

liberate [líbərèit]   *vt.* 자유롭게 만들다

图 grant freedom to

图 extricate, release, disengage, unloose, free

예 *The students liberated their slaves upon graduating from the university.*

---

preserve [prizə́:rv]   *vt.* 보호하다

图 keep in safety and protect from harm, decay, loss, or destruction

图 protect, keep, retain, conserve, maintain

예 *We preserve these archeological findings.*

---

maintenance [méintənəns]   *n.* 유지, 부양

图 the act of sustaining life by food or providing a means of subsistence

图 sustenance, support, preservation, conservation, upkeep

예 *They were in want of maintenance.*

---

merchandise [mə́:rtʃəndaiz]   *n.* 상품

图 commodities offered for sale

图 goods, product, ware, commodity, staple

예 *Good business depends on having good merchandise.*

personal [pé:rsənl]
a. 개인의

图 concerning or affecting a particular person or his or her private life and personality

동 private, own, particular, subjective, individual

예 *Do not use for your personal use.*

---

commitment [kəmitmənt]
n. 의무, 책임

图 an engagement by contract involving financial obligation

동 engagement, obligation, undertaking, pledge

예 *His business commitments took him to London.*

---

*Vocabulary/Expressions

insist [insíst]   *vt.* 강력히 주장하다

图 be emphatic or assert to be true

图 assert, persist, contend, press, urge

예 *The letter asserts a free society.*

---

mortgage [mɔːrgidʒ]   *n.* 저당

图 a conditional conveyance of property as security for the repayment of a loan

图 pledge, debt, loan, contract, deed

예 *mortgage loan*

---

heavy [hévi]   *a.* 무거운

图 of comparatively great physical weight or density

图 massive, hefty, weighty, ponderous, corpulent

예 *a heavy load*

---

inconspicuous [inkənspíkjuəs]   *a.* 눈에 띄지 않는

图 not prominent or readily noticeable

图 invisible, unnoticeable, imperceptible, unemphatic, indistinct

예 *He pushed the string through an inconspicuous hole.*

---

induce [indjúːs]   *vt.* 권유하다

图 cause to act in a specified manner

图 provoke, cause, bring, persuade, stimulate

예 *The ads induced me to buy a VCR.*

---

evaluation [ivæ̀ljueiʃən]   *n.* 평가

图 an appraisal of the value of something

图 estimation, assessment, rating, valuation, appraisement

예 *He set a high evaluation on friendship.*

tedious [tíːdiəs] *a.* 지루한

图 so lacking in interest as to cause mental weariness

图 dull, wearisome, tiresome, prosy, irksome

阅 *I spent tedious days on the train.*

---

invigorate [invígərèit] *vt.* 기운나게 하다

图 give life or energy to

图 strengthen, fortify, quicken, nerve, refresh

阅 *The cold water invigorated him.*

---

major [méidʒər] *a.* 주요한

图 of greater importance or stature or rank

图 meaningful, important, notable, main, principal

阅 *a major artist*

---

staircase [stέərkèis] *n.* 계단

图 a way of access (upward and downward) consisting of a set of steps

图 stairway, steps, ladder

阅 *moving staircase*

---

downturn [dauntə̀ːrn] *n.* 하강

图 a worsening of business or economic activity

图 worsening, lessening, downgrade, abatement, descent

阅 *The market took a downturn.*

---

sanitation [sæ̀nətei∫ən] *n.* 위생

图 the state of being clean and conducive to health

图 cleanliness, asepsis, hygiene, disinfection

阅 *urban sanitation*

invalid [ínvəlid]   *vt.* 병약하게 하다
图 injure permanently
동 disabled, handicap, sickly, incapacitate, weak
예 *He was invalided in a car accident.*

steer [stíər]   *vt.* 나아가게 하다, 이끌다
图 be a guiding or motivating force or drive
동 lead, conduct, guide, manage, direct
예 *The teacher steered the gifted students towards the more challenging courses.*

mind [màind]   *n.* 의견
图 an opinion formed by judging something
동 opinion, idea, notion, judgement, thought
예 *She changed her mind.*

lumber [lʌ́mbər]   *n.* 재목
图 the wood of trees cut and prepared for use as building material
동 hardwood, log, timber, beam, wood
예 *seasoned lumber*

repugnant [ripʌ́gnənt]   *a.* 비위에 맞지 않는
图 offensive to the mind
동 loathsome, detestable, obscene, repulsive, abhorrent
예 *repugnant behavior*

catch [kǽtʃ]   *vt.* 붙들다
图 take hold of so as to seize or restrain or stop the motion of
동 capture, grasp, get, take, seize
예 *Catch the ball!*

invincible [invínsəbl]   *a.* 무적의

- 医 incapable of being overcome or subdued
- 同 strong, unbeatable, inexpugnable, unconquerable, impregnable
- 例 *an invincible army*

---

client [klàiənt]   *n.* 고객

- 医 someone who pays for goods or services
- 同 regular, customer, buyer, patron, user
- 例 *He is my client.*

---

premise [premis]   *n.* 전제

- 医 a statement that is assumed to be true and from which a conclusion can be drawn
- 同 supposition, assumption, prerequisite, thesis
- 例 *On the premise that he has been injured we can infer that he will not to play.*

---

abrasion [əbréiʒən]   *n.* 마찰

- 医 erosion by friction
- 同 detrition, corrasion, graze, attrition, scratch
- 例 *multiple abrasions*

---

overhaul [ouvərhɔ:l]   *vt.* 분해검사하다, 분해수리하다, 정비하다

- 医 make repairs, renovations, revisions or adjustments to
- 同 inspect, examine, fix, repair, mend
- 例 *You should overhaul your car engine.*

---

annihilation [ənàiəléiʃən]   *n.* 전멸

- 医 total destruction
- 同 extermination, destruction, extirpation, obliteration, extinction
- 例 *Bomb tests resulted in the annihilation of the atoll.*

function [fʌ́ŋkʃən]   *n.* 기능

圐 what something is used for

图 purpose, ability, role, use, capacity

예 *The function of an auger is to bore holes.*

diminish [dimíniʃ]   *vi.* 줄다

圐 decrease in size, extent, or range

图 lessen, decrease, fall, reduce, abate

예 *The amount of homework diminished towards the end of the semester.*

relative [relətiv]   *a.* 비교상의, 상대적인

圐 not absolute or complete

图 comparative, related, proportional

예 *a relative stranger*

immigration [ìməgréiʃən]   *n.* 이주, 이민

圐 migration into a place (especially migration to a country of which you are not a native in order to settle there)

图 settling, exodus, migration, emigration, transmigration

예 *immigration office*

economic [èkənámik]   *a.* 경제의

圐 of or relating to an economy, the system of production and management of material wealth

图 commercial, fiscal, profitable, financial, economical

예 *economic growth*

bump [bʌmp]   *vi.* 충돌하다

圐 knock against with force or violence

图 crash, impinge, hit, strike, knock

예 *My car bumped into the tree.*

copy [kápi]   *n.* 복사

图 a thing made to be similar or identical to another thing

图 ditto, reproduction, imitation, replica, transcription

阄 *She made a copy of the designer dress.*

---

furnish [fə́:rniʃ]   *vt.* 공급하다

图 give something useful or necessary to

图 supply, purvey, provide, render, endow

阄 *We furnished the room with an electrical heater.*

---

steam [stí:m]   *n.* 증기

图 water at boiling temperature diffused in the atmosphere

图 vapor, exhalation, reek, fume

阄 *This train is driven by steam.*

---

remuneration [rimjuːnəreiʃən]   *n.* 보상

图 the act of paying for goods or services or to recompense for losses

图 repayment, compensation, reward, requital

阄 *adequate remuneration for his work*

---

scorching [skɔːrtʃiŋ]   *a.* 몹시 뜨거운

图 hot and dry enough to burn or parch a surface

图 sweltering, fiery, hot, burning, torrid

阄 *scorching heat*

---

skip [skíp]   *vt.* 뛰어넘다

图 cause to skip over a surface

图 bound, jump, leap, gambol, hop

阄 *Skip a stone across the pond.*

irrelevant [iréləvənt]　　　　　　　　　　　　　　*a.* 부적절한

图 having no bearing on or connection with the subject at issue

图 irrelative, immaterial, unimportant, impertinent, insignificant

예 *irrelevant allegations*

gift [gíft]　　　　　　　　　　　　　　　　　*n.* 타고난 재능

图 natural abilities or qualities

图 ability, capability, faculty, aptitude, talent

예 *He has a gift for playing the guitar.*

current [kə́:rənt]　　　　　　　　　　　　　　*a.* 현재의

图 occurring in or belonging to the present time

图 existent, contemporary, present, present-day, actual

예 *current events*

inland [ínlæ̀nd]　　　　　　　　　　　　　　　*a.* 국내의

图 towards or into the interior of a region

图 interior, domestic, inside, intestine, internal

예 *The town is five miles inland.*

horrible [hɔ́:rəbl]　　　　　　　　　　　　　　*a.* 무서운

图 provoking horror

图 frightful, awful, gruesome, dreadful, terrible

예 *War is beyond all words horrible.*

performance [pərfɔ́:rməns]　　　　　　　　　　*n.* 실행

图 of doing something successfully

图 execution, achievement, fulfilment, show, accomplishment

예 *They criticised his performance as mayor.*

document [dάkjumənt] *n.* 문서, 서류
因 writing that provides information
동 record, paper, report, writing, letters
예 *my documents*

currency [kə́:rənsi] *n.* 통화, 유통
因 general acceptance or use
동 dollar, cash, money, notes, circulation
예 *the currency of ideas*

authority [əθɔ́:rəti] *n.* 권위
因 the power or right to give orders or make decisions
동 domination, power, ascendancy, influence, prerogative
예 *He has the authority to issue warrants.*

continuous [kəntínjuəs] *a.* 끊임없는
因 without break, cessation, or interruption
동 incessant, continual, permanent, uninterrupted, ceaseless
예 *a continuous row of warehouses*

part [pά:rt] *vt.* 나누다
因 force, take, or pull apart
동 sever, separate, divide, split, disunite
예 *Moses parted the Red Sea.*

ambiguity [æ̀mbigjú:əti] *n.* 모호함
因 an expression whose meaning cannot be determined from its context
동 obscurity, indefiniteness, uncertainty, equivocation, polysemy
예 *Clear up an ambiguity.*

spend [spénd]   *vt.* 소비하다

图 pay out

图 expend, consume, squander, disburse, waste

예 *She likes to spend her money.*

---

intelligence [intélədʒəns]   *n.* 지능, 이해

图 the ability to comprehend

图 understanding, wisdom, cleverness, intellect, wit

예 *native intelligence*

---

*Vocabulary/Expressions

peel [píːl]   *vt.* 껍질을 벗기다
- 图 strip the skin off
- 图 strip, uncover, decorticate, pare, exfoliate
- 예 *I peel apples well.*

---

ceiling [síːliŋ]   *n.* 천장
- 图 the overhead upper surface of a room
- 图 dome, housetop, plafond, roof, vaulting
- 예 *He hated painting the ceiling.*

---

jump [dʒʌmp]   *vi.* 뛰다
- 图 move forward by leaps and bounds
- 图 vault, hop, leap, bound, skip
- 예 *Can you jump over the fence?*

---

salvation [sælvéiʃən]   *n.* 구제, 구조
- 图 a means of preserving from harm or unpleasantness
- 图 saving, deliverance, rescue, extrication, sustentation
- 예 *Tourism was their economic salvation.*

---

pollute [pəlúːt]   *vt.* 더럽히다
- 图 make impure
- 图 contaminate, befoul, defile, smirch, taint
- 예 *The industrial wastes polluted the lake.*

---

debate [dibeit]   *vt.* 논쟁하다, 토론하다
- 图 argue with one another
- 图 discept, discuss, controvert, dispute, moot
- 예 *We debated the question of abortion.*

extract [ikstrǽkt]   *vt.* 뽑다

圏 remove, usually with some force or effort

동 separate, derive, eradicate, withdraw, avulse

예 *He extracted teeth not to go the military.*

yield [jíːld]   *vt.* 산출하다

圏 be the cause or source of

동 afford, produce, give, provide, furnish

예 *Our meeting yielded much interesting information.*

perishable [periʃəbl]   *a.* 썩기 쉬운

圏 subject to destruction or death or decay

동 decaying, rot, transient, unstable, transitory

예 *Butter and fruit are perishable foods.*

baggage [bǽgidʒ]   *n.* 수하물

圏 cases used to carry belongings when traveling

동 trunk, luggage, valise, fortnighter, paraphernalia

예 *baggage office*

leaky [líːki]   *a.* 새는 구멍이 있는

圏 permitting the unwanted passage of fluids or gases

동 broken, punctured, cracked, faulty, split

예 *a leaky defense system*

confirm [kənfə́ːrm]   *vt.* 굳게하다

圏 establish or strengthen as with new evidence or facts

동 support, affirm, sustain, corroborate, substantiate

예 *His story confirmed my doubts.*

noise [nɔiz]
n. 소음

图 sound of any kind (especially unintelligible or dissonant sound)

屠 clamor, bang, din, buzz, hubbub, uproar

예 *He enjoyed the street noises.*

---

digest [didʒest]
vt. 소화하다

图 convert food into absorbable substances

屠 break down, assimilate, dissolve, ingest, absorb

예 *I cannot digest dairy products.*

---

teem [tíːm]
vi. 가득 차다

图 be abuzz

屠 abound, superabound, crowd, overflow, swarm

예 *The plaza is teeming with undercover policemen.*

---

confiscation [kànfiskéiʃən]
n. 몰수, 압수

图 seizure by the government

屠 seizure, forfeit, expropriation, sequestration

예 *the confiscation of illegal funds*

---

couch [kàutʃ]
vt. 말로 표현하다

图 formulate in a particular style or language

屠 utter, word, formulate, phrase, frame

예 *I wouldn't couch it that way.*

---

conception [kənsépʃən]
n. 개념

图 an abstract or general idea inferred or derived from specific instances

屠 concept, idea, notion, perception, intellection

예 *a vague conception*

---

rendition [rendíʃən]   *n.* 번역

뜻 an explanation of something that is not immediately obvious

동 interpretation, translation, version, performance

예 *He annoyed us with his rendition of parables.*

---

circumstance [sə́:rkəmstæns]   *n.* 상황

뜻 a condition that accompanies or influences some event or activity

동 situation, case, fact, occasion, condition

예 *the historical circumstance*

---

allocate [ǽləkeit]   *vt.* 할당하다, 배분하다

뜻 distribute according to a plan or set apart for a special purpose

동 assign, share, allot, set aside

예 *I am allocating a loaf of bread to everyone on a daily basis.*

---

consequence [kánsəkwens]   *n.* 결과

뜻 a phenomenon that follows and is caused by some previous phenomenon

동 event, result, effect, outcome, upshot

예 *He acted very wisely after the consequence.*

---

obligation [àbləgeiʃən]   *n.* 의무

뜻 the social force that binds you to the courses of action demanded by that force

동 duty, responsibility, commitment, liability, onus

예 *We must instill a sense of obligation in our children.*

---

energetic [ènərdʒétik]   *a.* 활기찬

뜻 possessing or exerting or displaying energy

동 active, vigorous, strenuous, dynamic, peppy

예 *an energetic group of hikers*

staunch [stɔ:ntʃ]   *a.* 충실한

医 firm and dependable especially in loyalty

동 devoted, steadfast, faithful, loyal, trusty

예 *a staunch defender of free speech*

---

surface [sə́:rfis]   *n.* 표면

医 the outer boundary of an artifact or a material layer constituting or resembling such a boundary

동 exterior, covering, outside, external, superficial

예 *The cloth had a pattern of red dots on a white surface.*

---

crack [krǽk]   *n.* 갈라진 금

医 a narrow opening

동 cleft, split, chink, rift, fissure

예 *He opened the window with a crack.*

---

divorce [divɔ:rs]   *vt.* 분리시키다

医 cease or break association with

동 separate, disjoin, split, disunite, disassociate

예 *She divorced herself from the organization when she found out the identity of the president.*

---

promising [prámisiŋ]   *a.* 장래성 있는

医 showing possibility of achievement or exellence

동 auspicious, likely, bright, hopeful, up-and-coming

예 *a promising new singer on Broadway*

---

impose [impouz]   *vt.* 강요하다

医 compel to behave in a certain way

동 force, enforce, inflict, ask, extort

예 *Social relations impose courtesy.*

interchange [intərtʃeindʒ]　　　　　　　　　　　　　　　　*vt.* 서로 교환하다
- 図 put in the place of another
- 동 replace, exchange, substitute, swop
- 예 *Synonyms can be interchanged without changing meaning of the context.*

deception [disépʃən]　　　　　　　　　　　　　　　　*n.* 속임
- 図 the act of misleading
- 동 fraud, cheat, delusion, trickery, hoax
- 예 *a deliberate deception*

soothe [súːð]　　　　　　　　　　　　　　　　*vt.* 달래다
- 図 cause to feel better
- 동 mitigate, pacify, mollify, appease, placate
- 예 *The medicine soothes the pain of the inflammation.*

discrimination [diskrìmənéiʃən]　　　　　　　　　　　　*n.* 차별
- 図 unfair treatment of a person or group on the basis of prejudice
- 동 differentiation, partiality, distinction, unfairness, discernment
- 예 *sexual discrimination*

bureau [bjúərou]　　　　　　　　　　　　　　　　*n.* (관청의) 국
- 図 an administrative unit of government
- 동 department, authority, office, agency, setup
- 예 *the Census Bureau*

plunder [plʌndər]　　　　　　　　　　　　　　　　*vt.* 약탈하다
- 図 destroy and strip of its possession
- 동 rob, harry, despoil, pillage, reave
- 예 *The soldiers plunderd the beautiful country.*

designate [dezigneit]
vt. 명시하다, 가리키다

- 图 indicate a place, direction, person, or thing
- 图 signify, show, indicate, point, denote
- 예 *He designated his opponents.*

sentence [séntəns]
vt. 선고하다

- 图 pass or pronounce judgement upon
- 图 condemn, judge, convict, doom
- 예 *He was sentenced to ten years in prison.*

infringement [infríndʒmənt]
n. 위반

- 图 an act that disregards an agreement or a right
- 图 contravention, violation, infraction, offence, transgression
- 예 *He claimed an infringement of his rights under the Fifth Amendment.*

assimilation [əsiməleiʃən]
n. 동화

- 图 the act of process of bringing to a resemblance, likeliness or identity
- 图 adaptation, familiarization, anabolism, absorption
- 예 *progressive assimilation*

tiresome [tàiərsəm]
a. 지루한

- 图 so lacking in interest as to cause mental weariness
- 图 tedious, weary, boring, exasperating, monotonous
- 예 *The performance was competent but tiresome.*

valuable [væljuəbl]
a. 값진

- 图 having great material or monetary value especially for use or exchange
- 图 costly, precious, rich, worthy
- 예 *a valuable diamond*

overdue [ouvərdju:]   *a.* 미불의

图 not paid at the scheduled time

통 owing, payable, unpaid, delinquent, outstanding

예 *an overdue account*

---

prestigious [prestídʒəs]   *a.* 일류의

图 having an illustrious reputation

통 famous, honored, influential, esteemed, reputable

예 *a prestigious author*

---

mingle [míŋgl]   *vt.* 섞다

图 bring or combine together or with something else

통 blend, intermix, compound, make up

예 *Resourcefully he mingled music and dance.*

---

homicide [háməsàid]   *n.* 살인

图 the killing of a human being by another human being

통 murder, killing, assassination, manslaughter, rubout

예 *justifiable homicide*

---

sick [sík]   *a.* 병든

图 affected by an impairment of normal physical or mental function

통 ailing, ill, morbid, diseased, unhealthy

예 *He was sick from the monotony of his suffering.*

---

depart [dipá:rt]   *vi.* 출발하다

图 move away from a place into another direction

통 leave, start, migrate, emigrate, go

예 *The train departs at noon.*

strip [stríp]   *vi.* 벗다

㊜ get undressed

㊜ undress, uncover, disrobe, denude, peel

㊞ *Please don't strip in front of everybody!*

---

imprisonment [impríznmənt]   *n.* 투옥

㊜ putting someone in prison or in a jail as lawful punishment

㊜ confinement, incarceration, captivity, duress, immurement

㊞ *the imprisonment of captured soldiers*

---

*Vocabulary/Expressions

painstaking [péinztèikiŋ]　　　　　　　　　　　　　*a.* 근면한

图 characterized by extreme care and great effort

图 diligent, industrious, scrupulous, conscientious, assiduous

예 *His painstaking efforts have been made to do it.*

---

plenty [plénti]　　　　　　　　　　　　　　　　　*n.* 많음, 풍부

图 a large number or amount or extent

图 abundant, ample, sufficiency, copious, profusion

예 *See the rest of the winners in our plenty passel of photos.*

---

downright [dàunràit]　　　　　　　　　　　　　　*a.* 솔직한

图 characterized by plain blunt honesty

图 candid, straight, forthright, straightforward, outspoken

예 *a downright answer*

---

break [bréik]　　　　　　　　　　　　　　　　　*vi.* 깨지다

图 become separated into pieces or fragments

图 crack, shatter, fracture, smash, separate

예 *The figurine broke into pieces.*

---

halt [hɔːlt]　　　　　　　　　　　　　　　　　　*vt.* 멈추다

图 stop from happening or developing

图 hesitate, cease, pause, interrupt, stop

예 *Halt the process.*

---

rent [rént]　　　　　　　　　　　　　　　　　　*vt.* 임대하다

图 engage for service under a term of contract

图 charter, hire, lease, engage, take

예 *Let's rent a car.*

familiar [fəmíljər]   *a.* 잘 알려진

뜻 well known or easily recognized

동 close, acquainted, conversant, intimate, accustomed

예 *a familiar figure*

---

boost [buːst]   *vt.* 밀어올리다

뜻 increase or raise

동 promote, advance, further, elevate, raise

예 *He boosts the voltage in an electrical circuit.*

---

pastime [pǽstàim]   *n.* 기분전환

뜻 a diversion that occupies one's time and thoughts (usually pleasantly)

동 entertainment, hobby, amusement, recreation, diversion

예 *She swims in her pastime.*

---

stability [stəbíləti]   *n.* 안정

뜻 the quality of being enduring and free from change or variation

동 constancy, durability, firmness, steadiness, fixity

예 *Early mariners relied on the stability of the trade winds.*

---

temporary [témpərèri]   *a.* 일시적인

뜻 not permanent

동 makeshift, transitory, impermanent, provisional, interim

예 *a temperary arrangement*

---

comfy [kʌmfi]   *a.* 쾌적한

뜻 providing or experiencing physical well-being or relief

동 comfortable, snug, convenient, easy, cosy

예 *comfy suburban houses*

evade [iveid] *vt.* 피하다

图 escape, either physically or mentally

图 escape, avoid, shun, elude, sidestep

예 *The thief evaded the police.*

safeguard [séifgà:rd] *vt.* 보호하다

图 make safe

图 protect, preserve, secure, defend, shelter

예 *I try to safeguard my rights.*

distressing [distrésiŋ] *a.* 괴로움을 주는

图 causing worry or anxiety

图 painful, sad, distressful, troubling, grievous

예 *a distressing amount of crime*

waste [wéist] *vt.* 낭비하다

图 spend thoughtlessly

图 lose, consume, squander, dissipate, misspend

예 *He wasted his inheritance on his insincere friends.*

regulation [règjuléiʃən] *n.* 규칙, 규정

图 a principle or condition that customarily governs behavior

图 law, adjustment, reg, control, rule

예 *It was his regulation to take a walk before breakfast.*

persecution [pə̀:rsikjú:ʃən] *n.* 박해, 학대

图 inflicting loss, pain, or death for adhearance to a particular creed of mode of worship

图 oppression, affliction, torment, infliction, torture

예 *religious persecution*

attorney [ətə́:rni]　　　　　　　　　　　　　　*n.* 변호사

㈜ a professional person authorized to practice law

㈜ lawyer, jurist, pleader, counselor, barrister

㈜ *I hire an attorney to solve the case.*

---

normally [nɔ́:rməli]　　　　　　　　　　　　*a.* 보통은

㈜ under normal conditions

㈜ ordinarily, generally, unremarkably, commonly, usually

㈜ *Normally she always comes late.*

---

tremendous [trimendəs]　　　　　　　　　　*a.* 거대한

㈜ extraordinarily large in size or extent or amount or power or degree

㈜ huge, monstrous, enormous, vast, colossal

㈜ *A plane took off with a tremendous noise.*

---

controversial [kɑ̀ntrəvə́:rʃəl]　　　　　　*a.* 논쟁의

㈜ marked by or capable of arousing dispute

㈜ contentious, disputable, argumentative, debatable, polemic

㈜ *a controversial decision on affirmative action*

---

slice [slais]　　　　　　　　　　　　　*n.* 얇게 썬 조각

㈜ serving that has been cut from a larger portion

㈜ portion, section, allotment, piece, segment

㈜ *a slice of bread*

---

applicant [ǽplikənt]　　　　　　　　　　*n.* 응모자

㈜ a person who requests or seeks something such as assistance or employment
　or admission

㈜ candidate, aspirant, postulant, suitor, petitioner

㈜ *an applicant for admission to a school*

uphold [ʌphould]   *vt.* 지지하다, 유지하다

뜻 keep or maintain in unaltered condition

동 brace, support, maintain, preserve, sustain

예 *Uphold the peace in the family.*

---

submit [səbmit]   *vt.* 제출하다

뜻 hand over formally

동 offer, hand, surrender, present, yield

예 *I submitted my resignation.*

---

carry [kǽri]   *vt.* 나르다

뜻 move while supporting, either in a vehicle or in one's hands or on one's body

동 transport, convey, take, bring, tote

예 *You must carry your camping gear.*

---

fragrance [fréigrəns]   *n.* 향기

뜻 a distinctive odor that is pleasant

동 odour, perfume, scent, aroma, redolence

예 *the fragrance of roses*

---

brief [briːf]   *a.* 간결한

뜻 concise and succinct

동 concise, short, compendious, succinct, terse

예 *He covered the matter in a brief statement.*

---

ordinance [ɔːrdənəns]   *n.* 법령

뜻 an authoritative rule

동 decree, order, edict, regulation, fiat

예 *city ordinance*

parallel [pǽrəlèl]   *a.* 평행의

医 being everywhere equidistant and not intersecting

동 alongside, collateral, lateral, aligned, side-by-side

예 *Parallel lines never converge.*

---

express [ikspres]   *vt.* 표현하다

医 give utterance to

동 utter, show, represent, articulate, reveal

예 *She expressed her disappointment.*

---

merit [merit]   *n.* 장점

医 any admirable quality or attribute

동 worth, advantage, strong point, excellence, virtue

예 *Working at lab has great merit to students.*

---

vigorous [vígərəs]   *a.* 정력적인

医 characterized by forceful and energetic action or activity

동 forceful, energetic, robust, sturdy, powerful

예 *a vigorous hiker*

---

jail [dʒéil]   *vt.* 투옥하다

医 lock up or confine, in or as in a jail

동 confine, imprison, gaol, immure, incarcerate

예 *The suspects were jailed without trial.*

---

crush [krʌʃ]   *vt.* 눌러 부수다

医 compress with violence, out of natural shape or condition

동 grind, squash, mash, press, squeeze

예 *He crushed an aluminum can.*

speculation [spèkjuléiʃən]   *n.* 사색

图 continuous and profound contemplation or musing on a subject or series of
   subjects of a deep or abstruse nature

图 contemplation, brainwork, meditation, reflection, deliberation

예 *The habit of speculation is the basis for all real knowledge.*

---

renew [rinju:]   *vt.* 새롭게 하다

图 reestablish on a new, usually improved, basis or make new or like new

图 renovate, recreate, refurbish, freshen, regenerate

예 *They renewed their membership.*

---

trend [trend]   *n.* 경향, 동향, 추세

图 a general direction in which something tends to move

图 direction, current, flow, bias, tendency

예 *the trend of the stock market*

---

reciprocal [risíprəkəl]   *a.* 상호간의

图 concerning each of two or more persons or things

图 common, respective, two-sided, joint, mutual

예 *reciprocal aid*

---

trickle [tríkl]   *vi.* 똑똑 떨어지다

图 run or flow slowly, as in drops or in an unsteady stream

图 dribble, ooze, leak, drop, filter

예 *Water trickled onto the lawn from the broken hose.*

---

belonging [bilɔ́:ŋiŋ]   *n.* 소유물, 재산

图 the property that pertains to someone

图 material, property, asset, goods, possession

예 *He is examining her belongings.*

---

distribute [distribju:t]

vt. 분배하다

医 administer or bestow, as in small portions

图 divide, share, allocate, disperse, apportion

예 *Distribute pocket money for the children.*

---

illegal [ilí:gəl]

a. 불법의

医 prohibited by law or by official or accepted rules

图 illegitimate, lawless, unlawful, illicit, wrongful

예 *an illegal chess move*

---

vend [vend]

vt. 팔고 다니다

医 sell or offer for sale from place to place

图 market, carry, peddle, sell, monger

예 *I vend my wares to earn money.*

---

declare [diklέər]

vt. 선언하다

医 announce publicly or officially

图 assert, proclaim, announce, pronounce, state

예 *The President declared war.*

---

outfit [autfit]

n. 조직, 기업, 회사

医 any cohesive unit such as a military company

图 firm, organization, company, enterprise, troop

예 *an insurance outfit*

---

optic [áptik]

a. 눈의

医 relating to or using sight

图 ocular, visual, optical, seeable, opthalmic

예 *optic inspection*

---

agree [əgríː]   *vi.* 동의하다

医 be in accord

동 accede, consent, permit, accord, concur

예 *We agreed on the terms of the settlement.*

---

repressive [riprésiv]   *a.* 제지하는, 억압하는

医 restrictive of action

동 oppressive, restraining, inhibitory, suppressive

예 *a repressive regime*

---

*Vocabulary/Expressions

Day 10

pay [péi]

vt. 지불하다

- 의 give money, usually in exchange for goods or services
- 동 defray, give, recompense, disburse, remunerate
- 예 *I paid four dollars for this sandwich.*

---

dexterous [dékstərəs]

a. 민첩한

- 의 skillful in physical movements
- 동 ingenous, clever, adroit, proficient, skillful, artful
- 예 *He is dexterous of hand and inventive of mind.*

---

stagnation [stægnéiʃən]

n. 침체, 정체

- 의 a state of inactivity (in business or art etc)
- 동 inactivity, calm, doldrums, standstill, torpor
- 예 *Economic growth of less than 1% per year is considered to be economic stagnation.*

---

capsize [kǽpsaiz]

vi. 뒤집다

- 의 overturn accidentally
- 동 overturn, invert, overset, upset, roll, topple
- 예 *Don't rock the boat or it will capsize.*

---

cultivation [kʌltəveiʃən]

n. 경작

- 의 production of food by preparing the land to grow crops
- 동 breeding, farming, nurture, culture, tillage
- 예 *Our land is being under cultivation.*

---

inadequate [inǽdikwət]

a. 부적당한

- 의 not sufficient to meet a need
- 동 inappropriate, unfit, incommensurate, unsuitable, inapt
- 예 *an inadequate income*

portable [pɔːrtəbl]   *a.* 휴대용의

- 医 easily or conveniently transported
- 동 movable, handy, conveyable, transportable
- 예 *a portable television set*

extend [ikstend]   *vi.* 뻗다; 이르다

- 医 span an interval of distance, space or time
- 동 elongate, stretch, augment, lengthen, continue
- 예 *My land extends over the hills on the horizon.*

roast [róust]   *vt.* 굽다

- 医 cook with dry heat, usually in an oven
- 동 bake, fry, grill, toast, broil
- 예 *My father roasts the turkey in the yard.*

confession [kənféʃən]   *n.* 자백, 고백

- 医 an admission of misdeeds or faults
- 동 affirmation, declaration, admission, profession, avowal
- 예 *The attorney is trying to extract his confession.*

prey [préi]   *n.* 먹이; 희생자

- 医 a person who is the aim of an attack by some hostile person or influence
- 동 victim, casualty, booty, loot, quarry
- 예 *the prey of a manhunt*

resignation [rèzignéiʃən]   *n.* 사직(서), 사임

- 医 the act of giving up (a claim or office or possession etc.)
- 동 retirement, withdrawal, abdication, renunciation, demission
- 예 *He gave his resignation to me.*

testimony [téstəmòuni]

n. 증언

- 围 something that serves as evidence
- 图 witness, statement, evidence, proof, attestation
- 예 *His effort was testimony to his devotion.*

upgrade [ʌpgreid]

vt. 품질을 개량하다

- 围 improve what was old or outdated
- 图 ameliorate, enhance, progress, advance, better
- 예 *I've upgraded my computer so I can run better software.*

facade [fəsá:d]

n. 정면, 외관

- 围 the face or front of a building
- 图 frontage, exterior, frontispiece, semblance, face
- 예 *the facade of a building*

dedicated [dédikèitid]

a. 헌신적인

- 围 devoted to a cause or ideal or purpose
- 图 committed, devoted, wholehearted, faithful, zealous
- 예 *dedicated teachers*

banquet [bǽŋkwit]

n. 연회, 축하연

- 围 a ceremonial dinner party for many people
- 图 feast, reception, festivity, treat, fete
- 예 *a banquet for the graduating seniors*

advisedly [ædvàizidli]

adv. 고의로

- 围 with intention
- 图 deliberately, purposely, intentionally, knowingly, wittingly
- 예 *He used that word advisedly.*

manure [mənjúər]   *n.* 비료, 거름

图 any animal or plant material used to fertilize land especially animal excreta usually with litter material

图 dung, fertilizer, muck, guano, ordure

예 *artificial manure*

---

concern [kənsə́:rn]   *vi.* 걱정하다

图 be on the mind of

图 regard, bother, occupy, tremble, worry

예 *I concern about the second Germanic consonant shift.*

---

surplus [sə́:rplʌs]   *a.* 나머지의, 여분의

图 more than is needed, desired, or required

图 extra, redundant, excess, supererogatory, superfluous

예 *He found some surplus change lying on the dresser.*

---

permanent [pə́:rmənənt]   *a.* 영구적인

图 continuing or enduring without marked change in status or condition or place

图 lasting, constant, steady, everlasting, standing

예 *a permanent secretary to the president*

---

nonchalant [nànʃəlá:nt]   *a.* 무관심한

图 marked by blithe unconcern

图 indifferent, unconcerned, careless, negligent, listless

예 *He drove his car with nonchalant abandon.*

---

languid [lǽŋgwid]   *a.* 나른한

图 lacking spirit or liveliness

图 dull, lazy, inert, slack, listless, sluggish

예 *a languid mood*

voucher [vautʃər]   *n.* 상품권

国 a negotiable certificate that can be detached and redeemed as needed

图 token, check, receipt, coupon, ticket

예 *luncheon vouchers*

---

lasting [lǽstiŋ]   *a.* 영속하는

国 existing for a long time

图 persistent, constant, permanent, abiding, durable

예 *I hope for a lasting peace.*

---

book [búk]   *vt.* 예약하다

国 arrange for and reserve (something for someone else) in advance

图 reserve, engage, bespeak, hold, preengage

예 *He booked a seat on a flight.*

---

impeccable [impékəbl]   *a.* 나무랄 데 없는

国 without fault or error

图 unblemished, blameless, immaculate, faultless, irreproachable

예 *impeccable logic*

---

promotion [prəmóuʃən]   *n.* 촉진, 장려

国 the advancement of some enterprise

图 rise, advancement, furtherance, forwarding, preferment

예 *His experience in marketing resulted in the promotion of his career.*

---

delinquency [dilíŋkwənsi]   *n.* 직무 태만, 과실

国 a tendency to be negligent and uncaring

图 remissness, carelessness, dereliction, heedlessness, negligence

예 *He inherited his delinquency from his father.*

---

incident [ínsədənt]   *n.* 사건

图 a single distinct event

동 episode, occasion, occurrence, accident, happening

예 *a touching incident*

---

sudden [sʌdn]   *a.* 돌연한

图 happening without warning or in a short space of time

동 abrupt, impetuous, unexpected, snap, unlooked-for, unforeseen

예 *a sudden storm*

---

moderate [mádərət]   *a.* 알맞은, 적당한

图 being within reasonable or average limits

동 temperate, modest, gentle, mediocre, reasonable

예 *moderate prices*

---

exhausted [igzɔ́:stid]   *a.* 다 써버린

图 drained of energy or effectiveness

동 worn-out, weary, fatigued, spent, tired

예 *She felt completely exhausted.*

---

amenity [əmenəti]   *n.* 기분에 맞음

图 pleasantness resulting from agreeable conditions

동 agreeableness, enjoyableness, delightfulness, mildness, pleasantness

예 *He discovered the amenities of reading at an early age.*

---

manufacture [mæ̀njufǽktʃər]   *vt.* 제조하다

图 put together out of artificial or natural components or parts

동 invent, construct, fabricate, make, produce

예 *That campany has manufactured small toys for 30 years.*

---

anticipate [æntisəpeit]

vt. 예상하다

图 regard something as probable or likely

图 expect, foresee, predict, previse, forebode

예 *The meteorologists are anticipating rain for tomorrow.*

---

resemble [rizembl]

vt. ~을 닮다

图 appear like

图 be alike, look like, be similar to, take after

예 *She resembles her mother very much.*

---

proclaim [proukléim]

vt. 선언하다

图 state or announce

图 announce, declare, exclaim, promulgate, pronounce

예 *The King will proclaim an amnesty.*

---

emblem [émbləm]

n. 상징

图 special design or visual object representing a quality, type, group, etc

图 symbol, sign, badge, ensign, token

예 *the Olympic emblem*

---

curtail [kərteil]

vt. 단축하다

图 terminate or abbreviate before its intended or proper end or its full extent

图 decrease, abbreviate, reduce, abridge, shorten

예 *Personal freedom is curtailed in many countries.*

---

reserve [rizə́:rv]

vt. 예약하다

图 arrange for and reserve (something for someone else) in advance

图 book, bespeak, hold, engage, preengage

예 *The agent reserved tickets to the show for the whole family.*

---

nutrient [njúːtriənt]　　　　　　　　　　　　　　　*a.* 영양이 되는

圀 of or providing nourishment

圐 nutritive, alimental, nourishing, alimentary

圙 *good nutrient stew*

attire [ətaiər]　　　　　　　　　　　　　　　　　*vt.* 차려입다

圀 put on special clothes to appear particularly appealing and attractive

圐 apparel, dress, garb, clothe, array

圙 *The young girls were all attired for the party.*

impertinence [impɔ́ːrtənəns]　　　　　　　　　　*n.* 건방짐

圀 inappropriate playfulness

圐 audacity, effrontery, impudence, forwardness, insolence

圙 *Please forgive my impertinence.*

corporation [kɔːrpəreiʃən]　　　　　　　　　　*n.* 주식회사

圀 a business firm whose articles of incorporation have been approved in some state

圐 company, enterprise, business, association, partnership

圙 *a public corporation*

launch [lɔːntʃ]　　　　　　　　　　　　　　　　*vi.* 착수하

다圀 begin with vigor

圐 start, establish, fling, plunge, throw

圙 *He launched into a long diatribe.*

economize [ikánəmàiz]　　　　　　　　　　　*vt.* 절약하다

圀 spend sparingly, avoid the waste of

圐 curtail, save, reduce, abridge, retrench

圙 *This move will economize money.*

anxiety [ǽŋzàiəti]   *n.* 걱정

囷 a relatively permanent state of worry and nervousness occurring in a variety of mental disorders

동 solicitude, concern, inquietude, tension, worry

예 *acute anxiety*

expert [ekspə:rt]   *n.* 전문가

囷 a person with special knowledge or ability who performs skillfully

동 adept, master, proficient, specialist, connoisseur

예 *This professor is an acknowledged recognized expert.*

*Vocabulary/Expressions

Day 11

formidable [fɔ:rmidəbl] *a.* 무서운
图 inspiring fear
图 frightful, awful, dreadful, horrible, terrible
예 *the formidable prospect of major surgery*

alternative [ɔːltə́:rnətiv] *n.* 대안
图 one of a number of things from which only one can be chosen
图 choice, option, selection, pick, redundancy
예 *What alternative do I have?*

allowance [əlauəns] *n.* 수당, 급여액, 용돈
图 an amount granted as during a given period
图 allocation, wage, fee, salary, stipend
예 *I think a child's allowance should not be too generous.*

wane [wéin] *vi.* 작아지다
图 grow smaller
图 decrease, lessen, diminish, recede, decline
예 *Interest in the project has waned.*

depression [dipreʃən] *n.* 우울
图 a mental state characterized by a pessimistic sense of inadequacy and a despondent lack of activity
图 gloom, despair, melancholy, abjectness, desolation
예 *manic depression*

lay [léi] *vt.* 놓다, 눕히다
图 put into a certain place or abstract location
图 pose, place, put, set, position
예 *Lay your things here.*

94

dreary [dríəri]　　　　　　　　　　　　　　　*a.* 지루한, 황량한

園 lacking in liveliness or charm or surprise

園 cheerless, gloomy, drab, lugubrious, somber

園 *a series of dreary dinner parties*

---

impoverish [impávəriʃ]　　　　　　*vt.* 가난하게 하다, 피폐하게 하다

園 make poor

園 beggar, pauperize, deplete, exhaust, ruin

園 *The event impoverished his memory.*

---

admission [ædmiʃən]　　　　　　　　　　　　　　*n.* 입장

園 the act of admitting someone to enter

園 entree, ingress, entrance, permission, admittance

園 *The surgery was performed on his second admission to the clinic.*

---

potential [pətenʃəl]　　　　　　　　　　　　　　*a.* 가능한

園 existing in possibility

園 possible, contingent, feasible, eventual, likely

園 *potential uses of nuclear power*

---

swing [swiŋ]　　　　　　　　　　　　　　　　　*vi.* 흔들리다

園 move or walk in a swinging or swaying manner

園 sway, shake, pendulate, dangle, oscillate

園 *He swung back in the swing.*

---

client [klàiənt]　　　　　　　　　　　　　　　　*n.* 고객

園 someone who pays for goods or services

園 buyer, patron, customer, regular, user

園 *He is my client.*

---

depress [diprés] *vt.* 낙담시키다

图 lower someone's spirits

图 deject, sadden, weaken, mortify, enervate

예 *These news depressed her.*

persuade [pərswéid] *vt.* 설득하다

图 cause somebody to adopt a certain position, belief, or course of action

图 convince, induce, coax, prevail, argue

예 *You can't persuade me to buy this ugly vase!*

extremist [ikstrí:mist] *a.* 과격한

图 (used of opinions and actions) far beyond the norm

图 ultra, extreme, radical, immovable, ultraconservative

예 *extremist political views*

exotic [igzátik] *a.* 이국적인

图 being or from or characteristic of another place or part of the world

图 strange, alien, foreign, peregrine, outlandish

예 *exotic plants in a greenhouse*

crash [krǽʃ] *vt.* 와장창 바수다

图 break violently or noisily

图 smash, break, shatter, disintegrate, splinter

예 *Who crashed this box?*

subscriber [səbskràibər] *n.* 기부자

图 someone who contributes (or promises to contribute) a sum of money

图 backer, donator, contributor, supporter

예 *He is a regular subscriber to our organization.*

storage [stɔ́ːridʒ] *n.* 저장

医 a depository for goods

圈 stockpile, ambry, store, entrepot, storehouse

例 *Storages were built close to the docks.*

---

compulsory [kəmpʌ́lsəri] *a.* 강제적인

医 required by rule

圈 mandatory, compulsive, obligatory, binding, coercive

例 *In most schools physical education is compulsory.*

---

observance [əbzə́ːrvəns] *n.* 준수

医 conformity with law or custom or practice etc

圈 obedience, awareness, fidelity, keeping, cognizance

例 *a religious observance*

---

reckless [réklis] *a.* 무모한

医 marked by defiant disregard for danger or consequences

圈 audacious, daring, adventurous, carefree, imprudent

例 *a reckless driver*

---

reluctant [rilʌ́ktənt] *a.* 마음 내키지 않는

医 unwillingness to do something contrary to your custom

圈 unwilling, unenthusiastic, indifferent, hesitant, discouraged

例 *a reluctant smile*

---

authority [əθɔ́ːrəti] *n.* 권위

医 the power or right to give orders or make decisions

圈 power, control, right, domination, influence, prerogative

例 *He has the authority to issue warrants.*

handle [hǽndl]   *vt.* 다루다
圀 interact in a certain way
동 care, deal, operate, manipulate, treat
예 *Handle that glass with caution, please.*

contagion [kənteidʒən]   *n.* 전염, 감염
圀 an incident in which an infectious disease is transmitted
동 taint, contamination, infection, plague, transmission
예 *contagion risk*

fluctuation [flʌktʃuéiʃən]   *n.* 변동
圀 the quality of being unsteady and subject to changes
동 variation, change, inconstancy, oscillation, vacillation, wavering
예 *He kept a record of price fluctuations.*

command [kəmǽnd]   *vt.* 명령하다
圀 make someone do something
동 direct, order, dominate, bid, enjoin
예 *The author commands a fair hearing from his readers.*

broil [brɔil]   *vt.* 굽다
圀 cook under a broiler
동 bake, fry, grill, roast, burn
예 *He is broiling fishes.*

dissolve [dizálv]   *vt.* 용해하다
圀 cause to go into a solution
동 resolve, disband, fuse, melt, thaw
예 *The recipe says that we should dissolve a cup of sugar in two cups of water.*

perceive [pərsíːv]   *vt.* 지각하다

图 become aware of through the senses

图 comprehend, notice, realize, discern, see

예 *I could perceive the ship coming over the horizon.*

---

saving [séiviŋ]   *a.* 절약하는, 검소한

图 characterized by thriftiness

图 economical, sparing, frugal, provident, thrifty

예 *I'm saving money for my tuition.*

---

influence [influəns]   *vt.* 영향을 끼치다

图 have and exert influence or effect

图 affect, sway, impel, operate, work

예 *The artist's work influenced the young painter.*

---

somber [sámbər]   *a.* 어둠침침한

图 lacking brightness or color

图 dark, murky, dismal, gloomy, tenebrous

예 *somber Puritan grey*

---

drop [dráp]   *vt.* 떨어뜨리다

图 let fall to the ground

图 dribble, lower, sink, drip, trickle

예 *Don't drop the dishes.*

---

tart [táːrt]   *a.* 신랄한

图 harsh

图 pungent, bitter, sharp, poignant, acrid

예 *tart criticism*

---

obese [oubíːs] *a.* 지나치게 살찐

뜻 excessively fat

동 plump, corpulent, fat, pursy, stout

예 *obese people*

---

infrastructure [infrəstrʌktʃər] *n.* 기반

뜻 the basic structure or features of a system or organization

동 base, footing, groundwork, foundation, underpinning

예 *The industrial infrastructure of Japan has developed a lot.*

---

consensus [kənsensəs] *n.* 일치, 합의

뜻 agreement in the judgment or opinion reached by a group as a whole

동 concurrence, accord, consent, unanimity, concord

예 *Those rights and obligations are based on an unstated consensus.*

---

envelope [énvəlòup] *n.* 봉투, 외피

뜻 any wrapper or covering

동 casing, jacket, sheath, cover, wrapper

예 *The spacecraft detected an envelope of gas around the comet.*

---

arguable [áːrgjuəbl] *a.* 논쟁의 여지가 있는

뜻 open to argument or debate

동 controversial, debatable, questionable, disputable, moot

예 *That is a arguable question.*

---

register [redʒistər] *n.* 등록부

뜻 an official written record of names or events or transactions

동 record, entry, roll, list, registry

예 *army register*

---

scan [skǽn]   *vt.* 자세히 조사하다

图 examine minutely or intensely

图 check, investigate, search, examine, survey

예 *The surgeon scanned the X-ray of the patient.*

---

leftover [léftòuvər]   *a.* 나머지의

图 not used up

图 residual, surplus, remaining, unexpended

예 *leftover meatloaf*

---

contaminate [kəntǽməneit]   *vt.* 오염시키다

图 make impure

图 defile, foul, sully, pollute, taint

예 *The industrial wastes contaminated the lake.*

---

competent [kámpətənt]   *a.* 유능한

图 properly or sufficiently qualified or capable or efficient

图 qualified, able, proficient, skilled, sufficient

예 *a competent typist*

---

conflict [kánflikt]   *n.* 투쟁

图 an open clash between two opposing groups or individuals

图 warfare, battle, contest, fight, struggle

예 *The harder the conflict the more glorious the triumph.*

---

preferable [préfərəbl]   *a.* 오히려 나은

图 more desirable than another

图 better, desirable, preferred, favored, preferential

예 *Coffee is preferable to tea.*

confess [kənfés] *vt.* 자백하다

㈜ admit to a wrongdoing

㈜ acknowledge, profess, admit, concede, recognize

㈜ *She confessed that she had taken the money.*

---

complimentary [kàmpləméntəri] *a.* 무료의

㈜ costing nothing

㈜ chargeless, free, gratis, costless, gratuitous

㈜ *complimentary admission*

---

*Vocabulary/Expressions

penalty [pénəlti]   *n.* 형벌

医 the act of punishing

동 punishment, castigation, retribution, amercement

예 *death penalty*

---

marine [məri:n]   *a.* 바다의

医 of or relating to the sea

동 maritime, aquatic, coastal, Neptunian, oceanic

예 *marine explorations*

---

chief [tʃí:f]   *n.* 장, 우두머리

医 a person who exercises control over workers

동 boss, director, commander, leader, headman

예 *If you want to leave early, you have to ask the chief.*

---

explosion [iksplóuʒən]   *n.* 폭발

医 the act of bursting

동 burst, outbreak, detonation, eruption, outburst

예 *The explosion of the firecrackers awoke the children.*

---

check [tʃék]   *vt.* 조사하다, 점검하다

医 examine so as to determine accuracy, quality, or condition

동 analyze, inspect, examine, investigate, scrutinize

예 *Check out the engine.*

---

sensible [sénsəbl]   *a.* 분별있는

医 showing reason and sound judgement

동 judicious, reasonable, wise, perceptible, rational

예 *a sensible choice*

cost [kɔːst]
n. 비용

图 value measured by what must be given or done or undergone to obtain something

图 charge, price, rate, expense, fee

예 *The cost in human life was enormous.*

---

rescue [réskjuː]
vt. 구출하다

图 free from harm or evil

图 save, redeem, salvage, retrieve

예 *Please rescue that sunken ship!*

---

dissipation [dìsəpéiʃən]
n. 소산, 분해

图 breaking up and scattering by dispersion

图 dispersal, scattering, disintegration, emission, waste

예 *the dissipation of the mist*

---

observe [əbzə́ːrv]
vt. 관찰하다

图 follow with the eyes or the mind

图 watch, keep, notice, perceive, remark

예 *She observed the men with the binoculars.*

---

negotiable [nigóuʃiəbl]
a. 양도할 수 있는

图 legally transferable to the ownership of another

图 transferable, assignable, debatable, conveyable, passable

예 *negotiable bonds*

---

refer [rifə́ːr]
vi. 관련되다

图 be relevant to

图 apply, relate, concern, pertain, touch

예 *There were lots of questions referring to her talk.*

---

discipline [dísəplin]   *vt.* 훈련하다

圀 develop behavior by instruction and practice

통 raise, train, chastise, school, punish

예 *Parents must discipline their children.*

---

sample [sǽmpl]   *n.* 견본

圀 small part of something intended as representative of the whole

통 example, instance, specimen, type, model

예 *I always buy things by sample.*

---

expiration [ekspərei∫ən]   *n.* 만기

圀 coming to an end of a contract period

통 cessation, expiry, closing, termination, conclusion

예 *the expiration of the driver's license*

---

recommend [rekəmend]   *vt.* 추천하다, 주장하다

圀 push for something

통 advise, commend, suggest, urge, counsel

예 *The travel agent recommended strongly that we not travel on Thanksgiving Day.*

---

combine [kəmbàin]   *vt.* 결합시키다

圀 put or add together

통 incorporate, amalgamate, connect, mix, unite

예 *I combined resources to make a new resource.*

---

invasion [invéiʒən]   *n.* 침입

圀 any entry into an area not previously occupied

통 attack, irruption, aggression, encroachment, foray, raid

예 *an invasion of tourists*

consent [kənsent]   *vt.* 동의하다
医 give an affirmative reply to
동 agree, comply, grant, subscribe, concede
예 *I cannot consent your invitation.*

quarantine [kwɔ́:rənti:n]   *vt.* 격리하다
医 place into enforced isolation, as for medical reasons
동 isolate, segregate, detach, insulate, restrict
예 *My dog was quarantined before he could live in England.*

junk [dʒʌŋk]   *n.* 고물, 허접쓰레기
医 the remains of something that has been destroyed or broken up
동 rubbish, trash, debris, lumber, refuse
예 *a junk car*

breach [brí:tʃ]   *vt.* 위반하다
医 act in disregard of laws, rules, contracts, or promises
동 infract, offend, transgress, violate, break
예 *He breached a law.*

generous [dʒénərəs]   *a.* 관대한
医 willing to give and share unstintingly
동 big-hearted, giving, noble-minded, benevolent, thoughtful
예 *a generous donation*

fringe [frindʒ]   *n.* 언저리
医 the outside boundary or surface of something
동 border, edge, margin, verge, hem
예 *He is on the fringe of the park.*

prohibit [prouhibit]   *vt.* 금지하다

- 國 command against
- 同 interdict, disallow, forbid, inhibit, impede, hinder, proscribe
- 例 *I prohibit you to call me late at night.*

implement [impləmənt]   *n.* 도구

- 國 instrumentation a piece of equipment or tool used to effect an end
- 同 apparatus, gadget, device, tool, utensil
- 例 *farming implements*

tear [tiər]   *vt.* 찢다

- 國 separate or cause to separate abruptly
- 同 split, break, lacerate, rend, rip
- 例 *Don't tear the paper.*

bulletin [bulətin]   *n.* 게시

- 國 a brief report especially an official statement issued for immediate publication or broadcast
- 同 announcement, publication, message, notification, statement
- 例 *an electronic bulletin board*

proponent [prəpounənt]   *n.* 변호자, 지지자

- 國 a person who pleads for a cause or propounds an idea
- 同 advocate, exponent, supporter, advocator, vindicator
- 例 *a proponent of Peace*

role [roul]   *n.* 역할

- 國 the actions and activities assigned to or required or expected of a person or group
- 同 function, duty, part, position, task
- 例 *He plays an important role in the drama.*

surrender [səréndər]   *vi.* 항복하다

뜻 give up or agree to forgo to the power or possession of another

동 relinquish, succumb, abandon, resign, concede, give up, hand over

예 *The last Taleban fighters finally surrendered.*

norm [nɔ:rm]   *n.* 표준

뜻 a standard or model or pattern regarded as typical

동 criterion, pattern, rule, model, standard

예 *the current middle-class norm of two children per family*

demolition [dèməlíʃən]   *n.* 파괴, 폭파

뜻 an event (or the result of an event) that completely destroys something

동 destruction, wrecking, wipeout, annihilation, explosion

예 *a demolition expert*

compartment [kəmpá:rtmənt]   *n.* 구획

뜻 a space into which an area is subdivided

동 department, section, stall, division, subdivision

예 *a smoking compartment*

execution [èksikjú:ʃən]   *n.* 실행, 집행

뜻 the act of accomplishing some aim or carrying out some order

동 fulfilment, accomplishment, enforcement, implementation, performance

예 *The agency was created for the execution of the policy.*

integrity [integrəti]   *n.* 고결

뜻 moral soundness

동 completeness, probity, honesty, integrality, wholeness

예 *They admired his scrupulous professional integrity.*

thrifty [θ rifti]   *a.* 검약하는

医 mindful of the future in spending money

동 saving, economical, frugal, provident, sparing

예 *He is thrifty with money.*

---

amateur [ǽmətʃùər]   *n.* 비전문가

医 lacking professional skill or expertise

동 inexpert, unskilled, novice, tyro, dabbler, dilettante

예 *He is an amateur but conscientious worker.*

---

lease [líːs]   *vt.* 임대하다

医 grant use or occupation of under a term of contract

동 engage, let, rent, hire, let out

예 *I am leasing my country estate to some foreigners.*

---

scare [skέər]   *vt.* 겁주다

医 cause fear in

동 frighten, intimidate, startle, horrify, terrify

예 *Ghosts could never scare her.*

---

inventory [invəntɔːri]   *n.* (재고)목록

医 a detailed list of all the items in stock

동 stocktaking, catalogue, list, roster, stock

예 *They carried a vast inventory of hardware.*

---

conclusive [kənklúːsiv]   *a.* 결정적인

医 forming an end or termination

동 decisive, peremptory, definitive, convincing, ultimate

예 *conclusive proof*

excess [iksés]   *n.* 초과, 여분, 과잉

뜻 a quantity much larger than is needed

동 superfluity, surplus, intemperance, surfeit, overplus

예 *excess of blood*

---

ruling [rúːliŋ]   *a.* 우세한

뜻 exercising power or authority

동 dominant, prevalent, regnant, predominant

예 *the ruling party*

---

drawing [drɔːiŋ]   *n.* 그림

뜻 an illustration that is drawn by hand and published in a book or magazine

동 draft, picture, design, sketch, draught

예 *It is shown by the drawing in Fig. 7.*

---

outstanding [autstǽndiŋ]   *a.* 눈에 띄는

뜻 having a quality that thrusts itself into attention

동 salient, arresting, prominent, noticeable, striking

예 *an outstanding rise in prices*

---

multiply [mʌltəplai]   *vt.* 증가시키다

뜻 increase in number; add quality to

동 augment, enlarge, propagate, raise, heighten

예 *He managed to multiply his profits.*

---

hardly [háːrdli]   *adv.* 거의~않다

뜻 almost not

동 infrequently, rarely, seldom, uncommonly, scarcely

예 *He hardly ever goes fishing.*

grouch [gràutʃ]   *vi.* 투덜대다, 토라지다

- 图 show one's unhappiness or critical attitude
- 图 murmur, complain, grumble, nag, repine
- 예 *We grouched about the increased work load.*

glance [glǽns]   *vi.* 흘긋 보다, 잠깐 보다

- 图 take a brief look at
- 图 peep, browse, peer, glint, peek
- 예 *She only glanced at the paper.*

*Vocabulary/Expressions

congestion [kəndʒestʃən]   *n.* 혼잡
- 圀 excessive crowding
- 圄 overcrowding, jam, overpopulation, surfeit
- 圆 *traffic congestion*

handout [hǽndaut]   *n.* 구호품
- 圀 giving money or food or clothing to a needy person
- 圄 donation, contribution, charity, dole, grant
- 圆 *She asked for a handout.*

sign [sain]   *vi.* 서명하다, 사인하다
- 圀 mark with one's signature
- 圄 inscribe, autograph, endorse, subscribe, underwrite
- 圆 *Please sign here.*

resign [rizain]   *vt.* 사직하다
- 圀 leave a job, post, or position voluntarily
- 圄 abdicate, relinquish, quit, renounce, vacate
- 圆 *She resigned the position when she got pregnant.*

lifetime [làiftàim]   *n.* 일생, 수명
- 圀 the period during which something is functional (as between birth and death)
- 圄 lifespan, existence, life, continuance
- 圆 *The battery had a short lifetime.*

settle [setl]   *vi.* 자리를 잡다
- 圀 place in a fixed or permanent condition
- 圄 arrange, lay, discharge, fix, place
- 圆 *Dust settled on the roofs.*

urgent [ə́:rdʒənt]   *a.* 긴급한

医 compelling immediate action

통 imperative, exigent, instant, pressing, clamant

예 *His house is in need of urgent reparation.*

---

confusion [kənfjú:ʒən]   *n.* 혼돈

医 disorder resulting from a failure to behave predictably

통 disorder, embarrassment, bewilderment, jumble, perplexity

예 *The army retreated in confusion.*

---

nourish [nə́:riʃ]   *vi.* 기르다, 영양분을 공급하다

医 provide with nourishment

통 cherish, feed, nurture, foster, sustain

예 *This kind of food is not nourishing for young children.*

---

illustrate [íləstrèit]   *vt.* 설명하다, 예증하다

医 clarify by giving an example of

통 explain, instance, exemplify, elucidate, interpret

예 *This compositional style is illustrated by this fugue.*

---

manufacturing [mæ̀njufǽktʃəriŋ]   *n.* 제조

医 the act of making something (a product) from raw materials

통 fabrication, making, formation, manufacture, production

예 *Manufacturing is vital to Great Britain.*

---

tremor [trémər]   *n.* 떨림

医 an involuntary vibration

통 quaver, trembling, quiver, shiver, vibration

예 *a slight tremor*

thaw [θɔ:] *vt.* 녹이다

图 become or cause to become soft or liquid

图 dethaw, melt, unfreeze, dissolve, unthaw

예 *The meat is thawed.*

---

overcast [òuvərkǽst] *vt.* 흐리게 하다, 어둡게 하다

图 become cloudy

图 cloud, obscure, darken, eclipse, overcloud

예 *Fall weather often overcasts our beaches.*

---

pier [píər] *n.* 부두

图 platform built out from the shore into the water and supported by piles

图 deck, wharf, dock, quay, wharfage

예 *Go into pier.*

---

concede [kənsi:d] *vt.* 인정하다, 용인하다

图 admit to a wrongdoing

图 acknowledge, accord, cede, confess, grant

예 *She conceded that she had taken the money.*

---

capacity [kəpǽsəti] *n.* 재능

图 the possession of strength, wealth, or talent

图 ability, talent, capability, power, competence

예 *a great capacity for growth*

---

common [kámən] *a.* 공통의

图 belonging to or participated in by a community as a whole

图 communal, normal, general, public, vulgar

예 *I and she have hobbies in common.*

lavish [lǽviʃ]   *a.* 아끼지 않는, 후한

医 very generous

동 bountiful, openhanded, munificent, prodigal, unstinted

예 *his lavish devotion*

---

strong [strɔːŋ]   *a.* 강한

医 having strength or power greater than average or expected

동 intense, robust, mighty, powerful, sturdy

예 *strong medicine*

---

counterfeit [kauntərfit]   *a.* 위조의, 가짜의

医 not genuine

동 fake, imitative, false, bogus, spurious

예 *counterfeit money*

---

testify [téstəfài]   *vi.* 증명하다

医 provide evidence for

동 attest, vouch, certify, give evidence, witness

예 *Her behavior testified to her incompetence.*

---

destination [destəneiʃən]   *n.* 목적지

医 the place designated as the end

동 aim, finish, purpose, goal, terminal

예 *A crowd assembled at the destination.*

---

increase [inkríːs]   *vt.* 증가시키다

医 make bigger or more

동 augment, extend, enlarge, grow, multiply

예 *The boss finally increased her salary.*

---

diminution [dìmənjúːʃən]   *n.* 감소

- 医 change toward something smaller or lower
- 동 cutback, lessening, reduction, abatement, decrement
- 예 *A diminution in the population is in progress.*

edify [édəfài]   *vt.* 계발하다

- 医 improve the morality, intellect, etc.
- 동 educate, instruct, teach, uplift, enlighten
- 예 *He likes to edfy himself by meditation.*

counterpart [kàuntərpàːrt]   *n.* 사본

- 医 a duplicate copy
- 동 copy, replica, duplication, reproduction, transcription
- 예 *He made a counterpart for the files.*

division [diviʒən]   *n.* 구획

- 医 one of the portions into which something is regarded as divided and which together constitute a whole
- 동 department, part, section, partition, separation
- 예 *the written division of the exam*

allocation [æ̀ləkéiʃən]   *n.* 배당, 배급

- 医 the act of distributing by allotting or apportioning
- 동 allotment, apportionment, distribution, appropriation, assignment
- 예 *food allocation*

default [difɔ́ːlt]   *n.* 태만

- 医 loss due to not showing up
- 동 dereliction, inadvertence, neglect, carelessness, remissness
- 예 *He lost the game by default.*

impartial [impá:rʃəl]   *a.* 치우치지 않은, 편견이 없는

图 free from undue bias or preconceived opinions

图 fair, neutral, unbiased, disinterested, unprejudiced

예 *the impartial eye of a scientist*

---

sector [séktər]   *n.* 부문, 분야

图 a particular aspect of life or activity

图 area, category, section, division, segment

예 *He was helpless in an important sector of his life.*

---

liability [laiəbiləti]   *n.* 책임

图 the state of being legally obliged and responsible

图 obligation, responsibility, accountability, duty, onus

예 *limited liability*

---

abject [ǽbdʒekt]   *a.* 비참한

图 most unfortunate or miserable

图 hopeless, poor, miserable, pitiful, wretched

예 *The most abject slaves joined in the revolt.*

---

retirement [ritàiərmənt]   *n.* 은퇴

图 the state of being withdrawed from one's business or occupation

图 pullout, superannuation, retreat, seclusion, withdrawal

예 *early retirement*

---

dismissal [dismísəl]   *n.* 해고

图 the termination of someone's employment

图 discharge, layoff, dismission, fire, removal

예 *an abrupt dismissal*

placement [pleismənt]

n. 배치

圀 the spatial property of the way in which something is placed

통 arrangement, organization, deployment, order, position

예 *the placement of the chairs*

adjourn [ədʒə́:rn]

vt. 연기하다

圀 close at the end of a session

통 defer, prorogue, delay, postpone, suspend

예 *The court was adjourned.*

vigorous [vígərəs]

a. 정력적인

圀 characterized by forceful and energetic action or activity

통 energetic, robust, forceful, powerful, sturdy

예 *a vigorous hiker*

install [instɔ:l]

vt. 설치하다

圀 set up for use

통 mount, place, set, furnish, settle

예 *Please install the washer and dryer.*

disorder [disɔ́:rdər]

n. 무질서, 혼란

圀 a condition in which things are not in their expected places

통 disarrangement, confusion, disturbance, mess, disarray

예 *The files are in complete disorder.*

household [hàushòuld]

n. 가족, 가정

圀 a social unit living together

통 housekeeping, family, house, family unit, menage

예 *He moved his household to Virginia.*

dump [dʌmp] *vi.* 내버리다

医 throw away as refuse

同 leave, cast, junk, let fall, discard

例 *No dumping in these woods!*

---

knowledgeable [nálidʒəbl] *a.* 지식있는

医 having extensive information or understanding

同 learned, knowing, enlightened, well-informed, smart

例 *a knowledgeable audience*

---

debris [dəbri:] *n.* 부스러기, 파편

医 the remains of something that has been destroyed or broken up

同 detritus, rubble, fragments, wreckage, dust

例 *debris surge*

---

taxation [tækséiʃən] *n.* 과세

医 charge against a citizen's person or property or activity for the support of government

同 tax, duty, tariff, levying, assessment

例 *a taxation office*

---

real [rí:əl] *a.* 진짜의

医 being or occurring in fact or actuality

同 genuine, existent, true, veritable, actual

例 *real humility*

---

boil [bɔil] *vi.* 끓다

医 come to the boiling point and change from a liquid to vapor

同 evaporate, steam, seethe, parboil, simmer

例 *Water boils at 100 degrees Celsius.*

complicated [kɑ́mpləkeitid]
a. 복잡한

图 difficult to analyze or understand

图 difficult, involved, complex, mixed, intricate, sophisticated

예 *a complicated problem*

interrogation [intèrəgéiʃən]
n. 질문, 심문

图 a sentence of inquiry that asks for a reply

图 quiz, hearing, question, inquiry, query

예 *He had trouble phrasing his interrogations.*

*Vocabulary/Expressions

superiority [səpìəriɔːrəti]   *n.* 우월

囷 at a competitive advantange

凮 advantage, preponderance, excellence, predominance, supremacy

囦 *He demonstrated the superiority of the ability.*

---

defective [diféktiv]   *a.* 결점이 있는

囷 lack in some respect

凮 imperfect, deficient, inadequate, faulty, incomplete

囦 *I returned the appliance because it was defective.*

---

agenda [ədʒendə]   *n.* 의제

囷 a list of matters to be taken up

凮 lineup, subject, matter, topic, schedule, plan

囦 *The matter is high on the agenda.*

---

anticipation [æntìsəpéiʃən]   *n.* 예상

囷 an expectation

凮 foresight, prevision, expectation, looking forward

囦 *Each of them had their own anticipations.*

---

superintendent [suːpərintendənt]   *n.* 감독

囷 a person who directs and manages an organization

凮 supervisor, manager, director, overseer, warden

囦 *the superintendent of schools*

---

radical [rǽdikəl]   *a.* 근본적인

囷 very important and great in degree

凮 basic, fundamental, cardinal, vital, primary

囦 *radical leaves*

---

bypass [baipæ̀s]   *n.* 우회로
图 highway that encircles an urban area so that traffic does not have to pass through the center
图 circuit, deviation, circumbendibus, runaround
예 *The bus takes the bypass.*

approve [əprúːv]   *vi.* 찬성하다
图 give sanction to
图 agree, permit, approbate, validate, commend
예 *I approve of his educational policies.*

internal [intə́ːrnl]   *a.* 내부의
图 happening or arising or located within some limits or especially surface
图 interior, indoor, inside, inner, inward
예 *internal organs*

accelerate [æksélərèit]   *vt.* 가속하다, 촉진하다
图 cause to move faster
图 expedite, precipitate, quicken, speed, hasten
예 *He accelerated the car.*

ruin [rúːin]   *vt.* 파멸시키다
图 destroy completely
图 demolish, spoil, devastate, wreck, destroy
예 *You have ruined my car by pouring sugar in the tank!*

manage [mǽnidʒ]   *vt.* 관리하다
图 be in charge of, act on, or dispose of
图 deal, govern, direct, handle, administer
예 *She managed her parents' affairs after they got too old.*

supplement [sʌpləmənt]
n. 추가, 보충

图 a quantity added

图 addition, extra, subsidiary, complement, appendix

예 *a calcium supplement*

---

violent [vàiələnt]
a. 격렬한, 난폭한

图 acting with or marked by or resulting from great force or energy or emotional intensity

图 fierce, severe, furious, intense, vehement

예 *a violent attack*

---

arrangement [əreindʒmənt]
n. 정돈, 배열

图 an orderly grouping (of things or persons) considered as a unit

图 alignment, disposition, array, display, lineup

예 *a flower arrangement*

---

suffering [sʌfəriŋ]
n. 고통, 고난

图 misery resulting from affliction

图 agony, hardship, distress, pain, misery

예 *He wants to die without suffering.*

---

reimburse [ri:imbə́:rs]
vt. 변상하다

图 pay back for some expense incurred

图 recompense, compensate, indemnify, offset, recover

예 *Can the company reimburse me for my professional travel?*

---

requirement [rikwàiərmənt]
n. 요구

图 something needed or necessary

图 demand, request, claim, urgency, requisition

예 *The requirements of his work affected his health.*

award [əwɔːrd]   *vt.* 수여하다

뜻 give, especially as an honor or reward

동 bestow, grant, confer, give, present

예 *He was awarded honors and prizes at graduation.*

---

cater [keitər]   *vt.* 조달하다

뜻 give what is desired or needed, especially support, food or sustenance

동 provide, gratify, supply, purvey, furnish

예 *The hostess catered lunch for all the guests.*

---

extensively [iksténsivli]   *adv.* 널리

뜻 in a widespread way

동 amply, broadly, largely, greatly, widely

예 *Oxidation ponds are extensively used for sewage treatment in the Midwest.*

---

effective [iféktiv]   *a.* 효과적인

뜻 producing or capable of producing an intended result or having a striking effect

동 operative, efficient, useful, competent, sound

예 *I want to learn effective teaching methods.*

---

metropolitan [metrəpálitən]   *a.* 도시의

뜻 relating to or characteristic of a metropolis

동 city, urbane, municipal, town

예 *metropolitan area*

---

admit [ædmit]   *vt.* 인정하다, 허락하다

뜻 declare to be true or admit the existence or reality or truth of

동 grant, allow, concede, permit, acknowledge

예 *He admitted his errors.*

affiliate [əfílieit]   *vi.* 특별 관계를 맺다, 제휴하다, 지부로 삼다

- 医 attatch (to) or united (with)
- 동 amalgamate, associate, combine, annex, consort
- 예 *The two colleges affiliated.*

---

resort [rizɔ́:rt]   *n.* 행락지

- 医 a frequently visited place
- 동 camp, harbor, lodge, spa, haunt
- 예 *seaside resort*

---

nasty [nǽsti]   *a.* 구역질나게 더러운

- 医 offensive or even (of persons) malicious
- 동 disgusting, offensive, abominable, obscene, loathsome, nauseating
- 예 *a nasty smell*

---

customer [kʌ́stəmər]   *n.* 고객

- 医 someone who pays for goods or services
- 동 client, patron, shopper, buyer, purchaser
- 예 *customer service*

---

novice [návis]   *n.* 풋내기

- 医 someone new to a field or activity
- 동 amateur, beginner, apprentice, tyro
- 예 *a novice driver*

---

murderer [mə́:rdərər]   *n.* 살인자

- 医 a criminal who commits homicide
- 동 killer, assassin, homicide, manslayer, cutthroat
- 예 *a mass murderer*

conform [kənfɔ́:rm]

vi. 따르다

图 adapt or conform oneself to new or different conditions

图 fit, adjust, comply, suit, adapt

예 *We must conform to the bad economic situation.*

devastate [dévəsteit]

vt. 황폐화시키다

图 cause extensive destruction or ruin utterly

图 destroy, ruin, demolish, ravage, waste

예 *The countryside was devastated by the enemy after the invasion.*

superb [su:pə́:rb]

a. 최고의, 훌륭한, 특히 우수한

图 of surpassing excellence

图 admirable, outstanding, marvelous, superior

예 *a superb actor*

implausible [implɔ́:zəbl]

a. 믿기 어려운

图 highly imaginative but unlikely

图 unbelievable, incredible, farfetched, improbable, unlikely

예 *an implausible explanation*

particular [pərtikjulər]

a. 특별한

图 unique or specific to a person or thing or category

图 uncommon, marked, peculiar, notable, special

예 *the particular demands of the job*

financial [finǽnʃəl]

a. 재정의, 재무의

图 involving fiscal matters

图 economic, budgeting, monetary, commercial, pecuniary

예 *financial responsibility*

stale [stéil]　　　　　　　　　　　　　　　　　　*a.* 싱싱하지 못한, 썩어가는

医 lacking freshness, palatability, or showing deterioration from age

통 faded, spoiled, musty, stinking, malodorous

예 *stale bread*

---

misty [místi]　　　　　　　　　　　　　　　　　　　　　*a.* 희미한

医 filled or abounding with fog or mist

통 filmy, obscure, dim, foggy, hazy, fuzzy

예 *a misty October morning*

---

maternity [mətə́:rnəti]　　　　　　　　　　　　　　*n.* 어머니다움

医 the quality of having or showing the tenderness and warmth and affection of or befitting a mother

통 maternalism, motherliness, parenthood, motherhood

예 *The girl's maternity made her invaluable in caring for the children.*

---

analyze [ǽnəlaiz]　　　　　　　　　　　　　　　　*vt.* 분석하다

医 consider in detail and subject to an analysis in order to discover essential features or meaning

통 investigate, examine, decompose, test, assay, inspect

예 *He analyzes the evidence in a criminal trial.*

---

disapproval [disəpru:vəl]　　　　　　　　　　　*n.* 안된다고 함

医 the act of disapproving or condemning

통 discontent, dissatisfaction, objection, disfavour, reprehension

예 *I shook my head in disapproval.*

---

durability [djuərəbiləti]　　　　　　　　　　　　*n.* 내구성

医 permanence by virtue of the power to resist stress or force

통 endurance, permanency, hardiness, stability, firmness

예 *They advertised the durability of their products.*

intersection [intərsekʃən]

n. 교차, 횡단

- 뜻 a junction where one street or road crosses another
- 동 crossway, interchange, crossroads
- 예 *an intersection point*

disabled [diséibld]

a. 불구가 된

- 뜻 incapable of functioning as a consequence of injury or illness
- 동 handicapped, crippled, incapacitated, invalid, maimed
- 예 *He was became disabled because of the war.*

bankrupt [bǽŋkrʌpt]

a. 파산한

- 뜻 financially ruined
- 동 broke, impoverished, destitute, insolvent, ruined
- 예 *a bankrupt company*

spill [spil]

vt. 엎지르다

- 뜻 cause or allow to run or flow from a container
- 동 shed, drop, slop, pour, splatter
- 예 *She spilled the milk.*

significant [signifikənt]

a. 중요한, 소중한

- 뜻 important in effect or meaning
- 동 important, critical, meaningful, notable, vital, momentous
- 예 *a significant change in tax laws*

analyst [ǽnəlist]

n. 분석자

- 뜻 an expert who studies financial data and recommends appropriate business actions
- 동 examiner, investigator, accountant, inquisitor
- 예 *investment analysts*

monetary [mánəteri]   *a.* 화폐의

- 图 relating to or involving money
- 图 financial, commercial, pecuniary, budgetary, capital
- 예 *monetary rewards*

---

fail [féil]   *vi.* 실패하다

- 图 be unsuccessful
- 图 fall, miscarry, break down, decline, neglect
- 예 *She failed to notice that her child was no longer in his crib.*

---

*Vocabulary/Expressions

Day 15

scholarship [skálərʃip] *n.* 학문, 학식
- 뜻 profound scholarly knowledge
- 동 learnedness, erudition, intelligence, knowledge, learning
- 예 *a man of great scholarship*

handily [hǽndili] *adv.* 쉽게
- 뜻 with no difficulty
- 동 fluently, conveniently, effortlessly, dexterously, readily
- 예 *She beats him handily.*

fresh [fréʃ] *a.* 새로운, 신선한
- 뜻 recently made, produced, or harvested
- 동 green, new, sweet, recent, young
- 예 *a fresh scent*

sordid [sɔːrdid] *a.* 더러운, 지저분한
- 뜻 foul and run-down and repulsive
- 동 dirty, corrupt, filthy, squalid, mucky, nasty
- 예 *I think that he is a very sordid soul.*

compensate [kámpənseit] *vt.* 보상하다, 배상하다
- 뜻 make amends for
- 동 reimburse, repair, recompense, indemnify, remunerate
- 예 *She was compensated for the loss of her arm in the accident.*

analysis [ənǽləsis] *n.* 분석
- 뜻 an investigation of the component parts of a whole and their relations in making up the whole
- 동 reasoning, assay, evaluation, interpretation, examination
- 예 *He makes an analysis of the event.*

indebted [indétid]　　　　　　　　　*a.* 부채가 있는

圈 owing gratitude or recognition to another for help or favors etc.

图 due, beholden, chargeable, liable, undischarged, owing

例 *heavily indebted company*

---

nomination [nàmənei∫ən]　　　　　　*n.* 지명, 임명

圈 the act of officially naming a candidate

图 appointment, delegation, designation, commissioning, selection

例 *the Republican nomination for Governor*

---

bilateral [bailǽtərəl]　　　　　　　*a.* 쌍방의, 양당의

圈 affecting or undertaken by two parties

图 interactive, respective, mutual, reciprocal, two-sided

例 *Bilateral FTA*

---

advocate [ǽdvəkeit]　　　　　　　*vt.* 옹호하다

圈 speak, plead, or argue in favor of

图 defend, plead, support, protect, uphold

例 *The doctor advocated a smoking ban in the entire house.*

---

recommendation [rekəmendei∫ən]　　　*n.* 추천장

圈 any quality or characteristic that gains a person a favorable reception or acceptance or admission

图 advice, endorsement, reference, approbation, testimonial

例 *Her pleasant personality is already a recommendation.*

---

notably [nóutəbli]　　　　　　　　*adv.* 특히

圈 in particular

图 especially, notedly, particularly, noticeably, remarkably

例 *Notably in the social sciences, the professors teach too much.*

expire [ikspàiər]
vi. 숨을 거두다

医 pass from physical life and lose all bodily attributes and functions necessary to sustain life

图 die, pass away, decease, end, perish

예 *The children expired in the fire.*

---

chamber [tʃeimbər]
n. 방

医 a room used primarily for sleeping

图 compartment, container, apartment, lodging, room, flat

예 *the Chamber of Horrors*

---

stingy [stindʒi]
a. 인색한

医 unwilling to spend

图 miserly, penurious, niggardly, parsimonious, skimpy

예 *She practices economy without being stingy.*

---

notification [nòutəfikéiʃən]
n. 통지, 공고

医 informing by words

图 advertisement, statement, announcement, intimation, communication

예 *prior notification*

---

progress [prágrəs]
n. 진보

医 gradual improvement or growth or development

图 improvement, advance, development, headway, evolution

예 *progress of knowledge*

---

stout [stàut]
a. 뚱뚱한

医 euphemisms for 'fat'

图 overweight, corpulent, portly, weighty, fat

예 *Men are portly and women are stout.*

investigate [invéstəgèit]　　　　　　　　　　　*vt.* 조사하다

医 conduct an inquiry or investigation of

동 inquire, examine, scrutinize, explore, search

예 *The district attorney's office investigated reports of possible irregularities.*

---

eruption [irʌpʃən]　　　　　　　　　　　　*n.* 폭발

医 a sudden violent spontaneous occurrence

동 outbreak, burst, irruption, explosion, outburst

예 *the eruption of hostilities*

---

prevail [priveil]　　　　　　　　　　　　*vi.* 우세하다

医 be larger in number, quantity, power, status or importance

동 dominate, preponderate, influence, overcome, predominate

예 *Hispanics prevail in this neighborhood.*

---

emanate [émənèit]　　　　　　　　　　　*vt.* 발산하다

医 give out (breath or an odor)

동 originate, arise, issue, proceed, exhale

예 *The chimney emanates a thick smoke.*

---

inappropriate [inəpróupriət]　　　　　　*a.* 부적당한

医 not suitable for a particular occasion etc

동 improper, unsuitable, inadequate, unbecoming, inapt

예 *Noise seems inappropriate at a time of sadness.*

---

ban [bǽn]　　　　　　　　　　　　　　*vt.* 금지하다

医 prohibit especially by legal means or social pressure

동 forbid, suppress, prevent, restrict, inhibit

예 *Smoking is banned in this building.*

---

saddle [sǽdl]   *vt.* (책임을) 지우다
뜻 impose a task upon, assign a responsibility to

동 weight, burden, load, tax, charge

예 *He saddled her with cleaning up all the files over the weekend.*

wage [wéidʒ]   *n.* 임금
뜻 something that remunerates

동 pay, fee, salary, remuneration, stipend

예 *Wages were paid by check.*

destroy [distrɔ́i]   *vt.* 파괴하다
뜻 do away with, cause the destruction or undoing of

동 ruin, wreck, annihilate, spoil, demolish

예 *The fire destroyed the house.*

stated [steitid]   *a.* 정해진
뜻 declared as fact

동 appointed, established, fixed, declared, set

예 *stated periods*

unload [ʌnloud]   *vt.* 짐을 내리다
뜻 take the load off a container or vehicle

동 disburden, offload, discharge, unship, dump

예 *He is unloading the truck.*

necessity [nəsesəti]   *n.* 필수품
뜻 anything indispensable

동 requirement, essential, need, requisite, necessary

예 *Food and shelter are necessities of life.*

injurious [indʒúəriəs]　　　　　　　　　　　*a.* 해로운

图 harmful to living things

图 dangerous, damaging, mischievous, hurtful, poisonous

예 *Smoking is injurious to the health.*

---

sore [sɔːr]　　　　　　　　　　　*a.* 아픈

图 hurting

图 irritated, aching, painful, raw, distressing

예 *the sore spot on his jaw*

---

deficient [difíʃənt]　　　　　　　　　　　*a.* 부족한

图 inadequate in amount or degree

图 faulty, scanty, insufficient, wanting, inadequate

예 *I was deficient in lung capacity.*

---

intend [inténd]　　　　　　　　　　　*vt.* 의도하다

图 mean or intend to express or convey

图 purpose, design, plan, aim, think

예 *What do his words intend?*

---

addiction [ədíkʃən]　　　　　　　　　　　*n.* 탐닉, 중독

图 being abnormally tolerant to and dependent on something that is psychologically or physically habit-forming

图 dependance, craving, enslavement, obsession, inclination

예 *drug addiction*

---

advisory [ædvàizəri]　　　　　　　　　　　*a.* 조언하는

图 giving advice

图 deliberative, helping, consultative, recommending

예 *His function was purely advisory.*

furthermore [fə́:rðərmɔ:r]   *adv.* 게다가

뜻 in addition

동 besides, moreover, farther, in addition, withal

예 *Furthermore, there's no sign of a change.*

---

somewhat [sʌmʰwʌt]   *n.* 약간, 다소

뜻 to a small degree or extent

동 a little, rather, little, slightly, more or less

예 *His arguments were somewhat self-contradictory.*

---

consume [kənsu:m]   *vt.* 소비하다

뜻 use up (resources or materials)

동 expend, dissipate, exhaust, spend, deplete

예 *This car consumes a lot of gas.*

---

disastrous [dizǽstrəs]   *a.* 비참한

뜻 having extremely unfortunate or dire consequences

동 catastrophic, fatal, unfortunate, pernicious, calamitous

예 *The battle was a disastrous end to a disastrous campaign.*

---

treaty [trí:ti]   *n.* 조약, 협정

뜻 a written agreement between two states or sovereigns

동 covenant, agreement, convention, pact, contract

예 *treaty powers*

---

denounce [dinàuns]   *vt.* 비난하다

뜻 accuse or condemn or openly or formally or brand as disgraceful

동 blame, charge, criticize, condemn, reprimand, reproach

예 *He denounced the government action.*

indication [ìndikéiʃən]   *n.* 지시, 암시

医 something that serves to indicate or suggest

图 symptom, mark, sign, token, indicant

예 *an indication of foul play*

---

reach [ríːtʃ]   *vt.* ~에 도달하다

医 come to a destination, either real or abstract

图 arrive, gain, stretch, extend, come

예 *The water reached the doorstep.*

---

insure [inʃúər]   *vt.* 보증하다

医 make certain of

图 guarantee, assure, ensure, secure, indemnify

예 *Preparation will insure success!*

---

equivalent [ikwívələnt]   *a.* 동등한

医 being essentially equal to something

图 same, similar, analogous, equal, identical

예 *His statement was equivalent to an admission of guilt.*

---

consider [kənsídər]   *vt.* 숙고하다

医 think about carefully

图 meditate, ponder, contemplate, reflect, ruminate

예 *They considered the possibility of a strike.*

---

controversy [kántrəvə̀ːrsi]   *n.* 논쟁

医 a contentious speech act

图 debate, argument, dispute, strife, contention, polemic, wrangle

예 *They were involved in a violent controversy.*

plead [plíːd]   *vi.* 간청하다

圀 appeal or request earnestly

圄 beseech, implore, entreat, request, beg

예 *I pleaded with him to stop.*

direct [direkt]   *a.* 직접적인

圀 straightforward in means or manner or behavior or language or action

圄 explicit, straightforward, outspoken, unreserved, categorical

예 *a direct question*

*Vocabulary/Expressions Day 16

ballot [bǽlət] *n.* 투표

뜻 a choice that is made by counting the number of people in favor of each alternative

동 poll, vote, referendum, election

예 *They allowed just one ballot per person.*

---

annual [ǽnjuəl] *a.* 1년의

뜻 completing its life cycle within a year

동 anniversary, yearlong, one-year, yearly

예 *a border of annual flowering plants*

---

approval [əprú:vəl] *n.* 찬성, 동의, 승인

뜻 the formal act of approving

동 authorization, consent, endorsement, sanction, assent, permission

예 *His decision merited the approval of any sensible person.*

---

consolidation [kənsὰlədéiʃən] *n.* 합동, 합병

뜻 the act of combining into an integral whole

동 merger, coadunation, integration, unification, combination

예 *a consolidation of two corporations*

---

equipment [ikwípmənt] *n.* 장비, 비품

뜻 an instrumentality needed for an undertaking or to perform a service

동 gear, devices, apparatus, kit, tackle

예 *audiovisual equipment*

---

established [istǽbliʃt] *a.* 확정된

뜻 settled securely and unconditionally

동 fixed, accomplished, entrenched, effected, vested

예 *That smoking causes health problems is an established fact.*

expansion [ikspǽnʃən]   *n.* 확장

图 the act of increasing (something) in size or volume or quantity or scope

图 extension, growth, development, enlargement, increase

예 *facility expansion*

affiliate [əfílieit]   *vi.* 특별 관계를 맺다

图 join in an affiliation

图 amalgamate, combine, annex, consort, associate

예 *The two colleges affiliated.*

salvage [sǽlvidʒ]   *vt.* 구출하다

图 save from ruin, destruction, or harm

图 save, rescue, redeem, salve, retrieve

예 *He salvaged her from a sunken ship.*

fragrant [fréigrənt]   *a.* 향기로운

图 pleasant-smelling

图 aromatic, perfumed, balmy, odorous, scented

예 *a fragrant tulip*

decree [dikríː]   *n.* 법령, 율령

图 a legally binding command or decision entered on the court record (as if issued by a court or judge)

图 edict, ordinance, order, rescript

예 *A friend in New Mexico said that the decree caused no trouble out there.*

calamity [kəlǽməti]   *n.* 큰 재난

图 an event resulting in great loss and misfortune

图 affliction, catastrophe, disaster, curse, misfortune

예 *The whole city was affected by the irremediable calamity.*

divert [divə́:rt]　　　　　　　　　　　　　　　　vt. 기분전환을 시키다
- 医 occupy in an agreeable, entertaining or pleasant fashion
- 동 entertain, amuse, gratify, beguile, relax, please
- 예 *The play diverted the ladies.*

---

apprehend [æ̀prihénd]　　　　　　　　　　　　　vt. 파악하다
- 医 get the meaning of something
- 동 catch, seize, grasp, understand, comprehend
- 예 *Do you apprehend the meaning of this letter?*

---

dweller [dwelər]　　　　　　　　　　　　　　　n. 거주자, 주민
- 医 a person who inhabits a particular place
- 동 inhabitant, resident, habitant, indweller
- 예 *a cave dweller*

---

match [mǽtʃ]　　　　　　　　　　　　　　　　vt. 경쟁시키다
- 医 set into opposition or rivalry
- 동 rival, contest, fight, compete, vie
- 예 *Let them match their best athletes against ours.*

---

complain [kəmplein]　　　　　　　　　　　　　vi. 불평하다
- 医 express complaints, discontent, displeasure, or unhappiness
- 동 grumble, protest, moan, repine, lament
- 예 *My mother complains all day.*

---

customs [kʌstəmz]　　　　　　　　　　　　　　n. 관세, 세관
- 医 money collected under a tariff
- 동 duty, tax, impost, tariffs
- 예 *customs-free*

---

consumption [kənsʌmpʃən]   n. 소비

图 the utilization of economic goods to satisfy needs or in manufacturing

图 utilization, depletion, exhaustion, use, expenditure

예 *The consumption of energy has increased steadily.*

---

inspire [inspaiər]   vt. 고무하다, 격려하다

图 spur on or encourage especially by cheers and shouts

图 encourage, exhilarate, animate, stimulate, exalt

예 *The crowd inspired the demonstrating strikers*

---

wholesome [hóulsəm]   a. 건전한, 유익한

图 conducive to or characteristic of physical or moral well-being

图 healthy, beneficial, salutary, good, sound

예 *wholesome food*

---

address [ədres]   n. 인사말, 연설, 강연

图 the act of delivering a formal spoken communication to an audience

图 sermon, lecture, speech, discourse, oration

예 *He listened to an address on minor Roman poets.*

---

practice [præktis]   vt. 연습하다

图 learn by repetition

图 exercise, drill, undertake, train

예 *Pianists must practice scales first..*

---

precisely [prisàisli]   adv. 정확히

图 indicating exactness or preciseness

图 exactly, accurately, definitely, correctly, just

예 *He was doing precisely what she had told him to do.*

deputy [depjuti]   *n.* 대리인

囹 an assistant with power to act when his superior is absent

图 representative, agent, proxy, substitute

倒 *My deputy went to the doing office.*

footprint [fútprìnt]   *n.* 발자국

囹 a mark of a foot or shoe on a surface

图 trace, footmark, vestige, footstep

倒 *The police made casts of the footprints in the soft earth outside the window.*

assembly [əsembli]   *n.* 집회, 회합, 회의

囹 the social act of assembling

图 gathering, aggregation, bunch, congregation, multitude

倒 *They demanded the right of assembly.*

fascination [fæ̀sənéiʃən]   *n.* 매혹

囹 the capacity to attract intense interest

图 attraction, enchantment, bewitchment, charm

倒 *He held the children spellbound with magic tricks and other fascinations.*

recognition [rekəgniʃən]   *n.* 인식, 인정, 인지

囹 the state or quality of being recognized or acknowledged

图 consciousness, realization, awareness, noticing, admission

倒 *The partners were delighted with the recognition of their work.*

reasonable [rí:zənəbl]   *a.* 적당한

囹 not excessive or extreme

图 moderate, understandable, fair, rational, valid

倒 *reasonable prices*

wonder [wʌndər]   *vi.* 이상하게 여기다, 놀라다

图 be amazed at

동 be astonished, surprise, be startled, marvel, admire

예 *We wondered at the child's linguistic abilities.*

---

truthful [trú:θfəl]   *a.* 진실의

图 expressing or given to expressing the truth

동 faithful, true, genuine, honest, veracious

예 *a truthful statement*

---

colleague [káli:g]   *n.* 동료

图 a person who is member of one's class or profession

동 associate, fellow, mate, companion

예 *The surgeon consulted his colleagues.*

---

medication [medəkeiʃən]   *n.* 약물(치료)

图 something that treats or prevents or alleviates the symptoms of disease

동 medicine, drug, medicament, treatment, remedy

예 *self-medication*

---

embark [imbá:rk]   *vi.* 승선하다

图 go on board

동 entrain, board, launch, ship, emplane

예 *He embarks for America in a steamer.*

---

compliment [kámpləmənt]   *vt.* 칭찬하다

图 say something to someone that expresses praise

동 praise, acclaim, felicitate, congratulate, appreciate

예 *He complimented her on her last physics paper.*

---

admonish [ædmániʃ] *vt.* 훈계하다

图 counsel in terms of someone's behavior

图 advise, reprimand, counsel, warn, exhort

예 *She admonished him to be quiet.*

---

determined [ditə́:rmind] *a.* 단호한

图 characterized by great resolution

图 purposeful, decided, firm, resolute, decisive

예 *a struggle against a determined enemy*

---

attitude [ǽtitjùːd] *n.* 태도, 자세

图 the arrangement of the body and its limbs

图 manner, posture, bearing, position, stance

예 *He assumed an attitude of surrender.*

---

despite [dispàit] *n.* 무례

图 lack of respect accompanied by a feeling of intense dislike

图 malice, disdain, grudge, contempt, rancour

예 *He was held in despite.*

---

migrate [màigreit] *vi.* 이주하다

图 move from one country or region to another and settle there

图 immigrate, move, emigrate, trek

예 *Many Germans migrated to South America in the mid-19th century.*

---

legitimate [lidʒítəmət] *a.* 합법적인

图 authorized, sanctioned by, or in accordance with law

图 lawful, valid, legal, rightful, licit

예 *a legitimate government*

---

ointment [ɔintmənt]

n. 연고

图 semisolid preparation (usually containing a medicine) applied externally as a remedy or for soothing an irritation

图 salve, cream, balm, unction, liniment

예 *He applied an ointment on my knees.*

---

exclusively [iksklú:sivli]

adv. 배타적으로, 오로지

图 without any others being included or involved

图 only, alone, merely, entirely, solely

예 *He works for Mr. Smith exclusively.*

---

mortify [mɔ:rtəfài]

vt. 굴욕을 느끼게 하다

图 cause to feel shame

图 humiliate, embarrass, abase, humble, chagrin

예 *He mortified his colleague by criticising him in front of the boss.*

---

assemble [əsémbl]

vi. 모이다

图 collect in one place

图 gather, meet, aggregate, forgather, rally

예 *We assembled in the church basement.*

---

neutral [nju:trəl]

a. 중립의

图 having no personal preference

图 impartial, unprejudiced, indifferent, unbiased

예 *a neutral observer*

---

burglar [bə́:rglər]

n. 강도

图 a thief who enters a building with intent to steal

图 robber, thief, picklock, housebreaker, cracksman

예 *a cat burglar*

barter [bá:rtər]　　　　　　　　　　　　　　　　　　　*vt.* 교환하다

图 exchange goods without involving money

图 change, exchange, trade, swap

예 *We barter wheat for machinery with foreigner.*

---

spew [spjú:]　　　　　　　　　　　　　　　　　　　　*vi.* 토하다

图 eject the contents of the stomach through the mouth

图 throw up, vomit, spue, puke, disgorge

예 *After drinking too much, the students spewed.*

---

*Vocabulary/Expressions

exit [égzit]   *n.* 출구
- 图 an opening that permits escape or release
- 동 outlet, way out, issue, egress
- 예 *He blocked the exit.*

devastate [dévəstèit]   *vt.* 황폐시키다
- 图 cause extensive destruction or ruin utterly
- 동 demolish, ruin, waste, ravage, destroy
- 예 *The enemy is devastating my country.*

retaliation [ritæliéiʃən]   *n.* 보복
- 图 action taken in return for an injury or offense
- 동 vengeance, reprisal, revenge, retribution, requital
- 예 *massive retaliation*

oppose [əpóuz]   *vt.* 반대하다
- 图 express opposition to
- 동 object, dissent, thwart, resist, withstand
- 예 *We oppose the ban on abortion.*

stipulate [stípjulèit]   *vt.* 규정하다
- 图 specify as a condition or requirement in a contract or agreement
- 동 impose, qualify, provide, specify, pledge, settle
- 예 *The will stipulates that she can live in the house for the rest of her life.*

recede [risíːd]   *vi.* 물러가다
- 图 pull back or move away or backward
- 동 retire, diminish, retreat, withdraw, regress
- 예 *The enemy receded.*

ailment [éilmənt]
n. 병

图 an often persistent bodily disorder or disease

图 disease, malady, infirmity, sickness, illness

예 *a serious ailment*

---

confident [kánfədənt]
a. 확신하고 있는

图 having or marked by confidence or assurance

图 assured, convinced, certain, trusting

예 *a confident speaker*

---

fatigue [fətí:g]
n. 피로, 피곤

图 temporary loss of strength and energy resulting from hard physical or mental work

图 tiredness, lassitude, overtiredness, exhaustion, weariness

예 *He was hospitalized for extreme fatigue.*

---

heal [hí:l]
vt. 고치다

图 provide a cure for, make healthy again

图 remedy, cure, recover, treat, cicatrize

예 *The treatment healed the boy's acne.*

---

payment [péimənt]
n. 보수, 보상

图 a sum of money paid or a claim discharged

图 payoff, fee, discharge, remuneration, disbursement

예 *The payment of work is very good.*

---

extent [ikstent]
n. 넓이

图 the distance or area or volume over which something extends

图 dimension, scope, range, degree, amplitude

예 *The vast extent of the desert made me astonished.*

stimulate [stímjulèit]　　　　　　　　　　　　　　*vt.* 자극하다

圐 cause to act in a specified manner

圐 provoke, incite, induce, encourage, spur

圐 *My children finally stimulated me to buy a computer.*

---

respective [rispéktiv]　　　　　　　　　　　　　　*a.* 각각의

圐 considered individually

圐 each, several, particular, individual, singular

圐 *the respective club members*

---

obsession [əbséʃən]　　　　　　　　　　　　　　*n.* 강박 관념

圐 an irrational motive for performing trivial or repetitive actions, even against your will

圐 fixation, inclination, compulsion, anxiety, bent, insanity

圐 *She has obsession to wash her hands repeatedly.*

---

singe [síndʒ]　　　　　　　　　　　　　　*vi.* 그스르다

圐 burn superficially or lightly

圐 burn, scorch, toast, parch, sear

圐 *My eyebrows singed when I bent over the flames.*

---

impair [impéər]　　　　　　　　　　　　　　*vt.* 약하게 하다, 손상시키다

圐 make worse or less effective

圐 weaken, deteriorate, harm, reduce, mar

圐 *His vision was impaired.*

---

initiate [iníʃièit]　　　　　　　　　　　　　　*vt.* 시작하다

圐 bring into being

圐 begin, start, launch, commence, originate

圐 *He initiated a new program.*

disconnect [dìskənékt]　　　　　　　　　　　　　　*vt.* 끊다
- 医 make disjoin or unfasten
- 동 dissociate, separate, sever, uncouple, disengage
- 예 *I remind you to disconnect the hair dryer after using it.*

treatment [trí:tmənt]　　　　　　　　　　　　　　*n.* 치료
- 医 care provided to improve a situation
- 동 cure, remedy, medication, therapy, healing
- 예 *beauty treatment*

cancellation [kæ̀nsəlei∫ən]　　　　　　　　　　*n.* 말소, 해제
- 医 calling off some arragement
- 동 deletion, erasure, annulment, abolition, rescission
- 예 *cancellation law*

conference [kánfərəns]　　　　　　　　　　　　*n.* 회의
- 医 a discussion among participants who have an agreed (serious) topic
- 동 argument, meeting, convention, congress, parley
- 예 *We have a conference with them.*

stubborn [stʌbərn]　　　　　　　　　　　*a.* 완고한, 고집센
- 医 tenaciously unwilling or marked by tenacious unwillingness to yield
- 동 rigid, obstinate, unregenerate, tenacious, unyielding
- 예 *a stubborn resistance*

suspect [səspekt]　　　　　　　　　　　　*vt.* 짐작하다
- 医 imagine to be the case or true or probable
- 동 guess, presume, misdoubt, reckon
- 예 *I suspect he is a fugitive.*

franchise [frǽntʃaiz]

n. 독점 판매권

图 a business established or operated under an authorization to sell or distribute a company's goods or services in a particular area

图 privilege, authorization, prerogative, dealership, patent

예 *franchise fee*

---

dispatch [dispǽtʃ]

vt. 죽이다

图 kill intentionally and with premeditation

图 murder, kill, eliminate, remove, slay

예 *The mafia boss dispatched his enemies on the spot.*

---

sue [súː]

vt. 고소하다

图 institute legal proceedings against

图 accuse, litigate, supplicate, entreat, prosecute

예 *I sue a person for damages.*

---

trouble [trʌbl]

vt. 괴롭히다

图 disturb in mind or make uneasy or cause to be worried or alarmed

图 disturb, bother, distress, annoy, harass

예 *Sorry to trouble you.*

---

instruction [instrʌkʃən]

n. 교육

图 the activities of educating or furnishing with knowledge

图 teaching, education, schooling, direction, precept

예 *He received no formal instruction.*

---

contamination [kəntæ̀mənéiʃən]

n. 오염, 더러움

图 the state of being polluted

图 pollution, infection, defilement, impurity, taint

예 *eye contamination*

charge [tʃɑ́:rdʒ]　　　　　　　　　　　　　　　*n.* 청구 금액, 요금

英 the price charged for some article or service

동 expense, cost, price, expenditure, payment

예 *the admission charge*

---

conspire [kənspàiər]　　　　　　　　　*vi.* 공모하다, 음모를 꾸미다

英 engage in plotting or enter into a conspiracy, swear together

동 plot, connive, machinate, scheme

예 *They conspired to overthrow the government.*

---

enhance [inhǽns]　　　　　　　　　　　　　　　　*vt.* 강화하다

英 increase

동 heighten, boost, increase, aggrandize, raise

예 *This will enhance your enjoyment.*

---

security [sikjúərəti]　　　　　　　　　　　　　　　*n.* 안전

英 the state of being free from danger or injury

동 safety, safeguard, protection, assurance, pledge

예 *We support the armed services in the name of national security.*

---

industry [indəstri]　　　　　　　　　　　　　　*n.* 근면, 성실

英 persevering determination to perform a task

동 diligence, dedication, assiduity, industriousness, sedulity

예 *His industry won him quick promotions.*

---

flourish [flə́:riʃ]　　　　　　　　　　　　　　　*vi.* 번창하다

英 make steady progress

동 blossom, thrive, bloom, succeed, prosper

예 *The new student is flourishing.*

conglomerate [kənglámərət]
vi. 응집하다

图 collect or gather

图 agglomerate, cumulate, amass, accumulate, gather

예 *Journals are conglomerating in my office.*

---

tune [tju:n]
vt. 조율하다

图 adjust the pitches of musical instruments

图 set, adjust, regulate, tone, key

예 *My piano needs to be tuned.*

---

apprehensive [æ̀prihensiv]
a. 우려하는

图 mentally upset over possible misfortune or danger etc.

图 afraid, worried, fearful, anxious, uptight

예 *He felt apprehensive about the consequences.*

---

disinterest [disíntərist]
n. 무관심

图 tolerance attributable to a lack of involvement

图 listlessness, apathy, unconcern, indifference, uninterest

예 *She watched the teacher with disinterest during the entire class.*

---

demonstration [dèmənstréiʃən]
n. 논증, 증명

图 the act of presenting something to sight or view

图 show, display, proof, manifestation, showing

예 *the demonstration of new data*

---

regular [regjulər]
a. 보통의, 규칙적인

图 in accordance with fixed order or procedure or principle

图 routine, normal, ordinary, typical, common

예 *regular meals*

publication [pʌbləkeiʃən] *n.* 출판, 발행

뜻 the act of issuing printed materials

동 issue, edition, publishing, release, promulgation

예 *The magazine started its publication in 1982.*

amend [əmend] *vt.* 개선하다

뜻 make better

동 ameliorate, improve, better, rectify

예 *The editor amended the manuscript with his changes.*

recurring [rikə́:riŋ] *a.* 되풀이하여 발생하는

뜻 coming back

동 periodical, recurrent, rotating, revenant

예 *a recurring dream*

expenditure [ikspenditʃər] *n.* 지출

뜻 the act of spending money for goods or services

동 consumption, expense, outgo, disbursement, outlay

예 *annual expenditure*

downpour [dàunpɔ:r] *n.* 억수같은 비, 호우

뜻 a heavy rain

동 drencher, shower, cloudburst, deluge, soaker

예 *a sudden downpour*

stifling [stàifliŋ] *a.* 숨막힐 듯한, 답답한

뜻 characterized by oppressive heat and humidity

동 suffocating, smothery, close, stuffy, sultry

예 *the stifling atmosphere*

entry [éntri]   *n.* 입장, 가입

囹 the act of entering or passing into

魯 enter, registration, enrol, registry, listing

예 *She made a grand entry.*

---

policy [pálǝsi]   *n.* 정책, 방침

囹 a plan of action adopted by an individual or social group

魯 guideline, strategy arrangement, scheme, rule

예 *It was a policy of retribution.*

---

*Vocabulary/Expressions

riddle [rídl]   *n.* 수수께끼
- 医 a difficult problem
- 동 mystery, brain-twister, enigma, puzzle, conundrum, question
- 예 *Children likes to answer a riddle.*

sluggish [slʌgiʃ]   *a.* 나태한
- 医 slow and apathetic
- 동 slack, lazy, slothful, indolent, tardy
- 예 *a sluggish worker*

finish [fíniʃ]   *vt.* 끝내다
- 医 come or bring to an end
- 동 conclude, accomplish, end, terminate, complete
- 예 *He finished the dishes.*

paste [péist]   *vt.* 풀칠하여 붙이다
- 医 join or attach with or as if with glue
- 동 glue, stick, gum, attach, fasten
- 예 *Paste the sign on the wall.*

endanger [indéindʒər]   *vt.* 위태롭게 하다
- 医 pose a threat to
- 동 menace, threaten, imperil, jeopardize
- 예 *The pollution is endangering the crops.*

suffer [sʌfər]   *vt.* 견디다
- 医 put up with something or somebody unpleasant
- 동 bear, endure, tolerate, digest, stand
- 예 *The new secretary had to suffer a lot of unprofessional remarks.*

grab [grǽb]   *vt.* 움켜쥐다

囲 take hold of so as to seize or restrain or stop the motion of

동 catch, grasp, seize, take, clutch

예 *Grab the elevator door!*

---

emerge [imə́:rdʒ]   *vi.* 나타나다

囲 come out into view, as from concealment

동 appear, show, turn up, emanate, arise

예 *Suddenly, the proprietor emerged from his office.*

---

welfare [welfɛ̀ər]   *n.* 복지

囲 governmental provision of economic assistance to persons in need

동 good, public assistance, prosperity, well-being

예 *She lives on welfare.*

---

build [bíld]   *vt.* 건축하다

囲 make by combining materials and parts

동 construct, frame, erect, form, make

예 *Some eccentric builded an electric brassiere warmer.*

---

option [ápʃən]   *n.* 선택

囲 the act of choosing or selecting

동 choice, selection, pick, election, alternative

예 *Your option of colors was unfortunate.*

---

scalding [skɔ́:ldiŋ]   *a.* 뜨거운

囲 heated to the boling point

동 torrid, boiling, fiery, hot, roasting

예 *scalding tears*

expense [ikspens] *n.* 지출, 비용
- 図 amounts paid for goods and services that may be currently tax deductible
- 图 cost, payment, expenditure, charge, disbursal
- 예 *accrued expense*

humanity [hju:mǽnəti] *n.* 인류
- 図 all of the living human inhabitants of the earth
- 图 humankind, people, humanness, society
- 예 *I really love him.*

resident [rézədənt] *n.* 거주자
- 図 someone who lives at a particular place for a prolonged period or who was born there
- 图 occupant, dweller, habitant, tenant, denizen
- 예 *a resident of a house*

interact [intərǽkt] *vi.* 상호작용하다
- 図 act together or towards others or with others
- 图 relate, connect, join, communicate, touch
- 예 *He should interact more with his colleagues.*

brutal [brú:tl] *a.* 잔인한
- 図 able or disposed to inflict pain or suffering
- 图 cruel, savage, vicious, barbarous, unrelenting
- 예 *brutal beatings*

collaborator [kəlǽbərèitər] *n.* 협력자
- 図 an associate in an activity or endeavor or sphere of common interest
- 图 partner, cooperator, associate, collaborationist, contributor
- 예 *The musician and the librettist were collaborators.*

employer [implɔiər]

n. 고용주, 사용자

뜻 a person or firm that employs workers

동 boss, master, manufacturer, entrepreneur, taskmaster

예 *employer-centered system*

---

feature [fiːtʃər]

n. 특징

뜻 a prominent attribute or aspect of something

동 attribute, property, idiosyncrasy, characteristic, trait

예 *Generosity is one of his best features.*

---

outlook [autluk]

n. 견해

뜻 a habitual or characteristic mental attitude that determines how you will interpret and respond to situations

동 perspective, attitude, viewpoint, angle, standpoint

예 *There are pretty different in outlook.*

---

equity [ékwəti]

n. 공평

뜻 fairness in determination of conflicting claims

동 fairness, justness, justice, impartiality, righteousness

예 *The judge recognized the equity of my claim.*

---

custodian [kʌstoudiən]

n. 관리인, 보관자

뜻 one having charge of buildings or grounds or animals

동 keeper, manager, supervisor, caretaker, steward

예 *land custodian*

---

population [pàpjuleiʃən]

n. 인구, 주민수

뜻 the people who inhabit a territory or state

동 populace, folk, people, citizenry, universe

예 *The population seemed to be well fed and clothed.*

confirmation [kànfərméiʃən]　　　　　　　　　　　　　　*n.* 확정

图 making something valid by formally ratifying or confirming it

图 affirmation, verification, ratification, sanction, corroboration

예 *the confirmation of the treaty*

---

enroll [inróul]　　　　　　　　　　　　　　　　　*vt.* 등록하다

图 register formally as a participant or member

图 enlist, recruit, enter, inscribe

예 *The party enrolled many new members.*

---

inconsistent [ìnkənsístənt]　　　　　　　*a.* 일치하지 않는, 모순된

图 displaying a lack of consistency

图 incompatible, contradictory, conflicting, discordant, inconsequent

예 *The contents are inconsistent with the latest scholarship.*

---

challenging [tʃǽlindʒiŋ]　　　　　　　　　　　*a.* 도전적인

图 requiring full use of your abilities or resources

图 ambitious, provocative, defiant, arduous, strenuous

예 *Performed the most challenging task without a mistake.*

---

extol [ikstóul]　　　　　　　　　　　　　　　　*vt.* 격찬하다

图 praise, glorify, or honor

图 celebrate, glorify, exalt, commend, praise

예 *I extoled the virtues of the students.*

---

cuddle [kʌdl]　　　　　　　　　　　　　　　*vt.* 꼭 껴안다

图 hold (a person or thing) close, as for affection, comfort, or warmth

图 embrace, hug, snuggle, enfold, fondle

예 *I cuddled the baby.*

fugitive [fjú:dʒətiv]　　　　　　　　　　　*a.* 덧없는

뜻 lasting for a markedly brief time

동 fugacious, momentaneous, ephemeral, fleeting, transient

예 *fugitive hours*

---

frugal [frú:gəl]　　　　　　　　　　　*a.* 절약하는

뜻 avoiding waste

동 economical, sparing, thrifty, provident, abstemious

예 *a frugal shopper*

---

reside [rizàid]　　　　　　　　　　　*vi.* 거주하다

뜻 live in a certain place

동 live, domiciliate, inhabit, dwell, occupy

예 *She resides in Princeton.*

---

motivate [moutəveit]　　　　　　　　　　　*vt.* 자극하다

뜻 give an incentive for action

동 stimulate, incite, propel, instigate, provoke

예 *This motivated me to sacrifice my career.*

---

prospective [prəspektiv]　　　　　　　　　　　*a.* 예상된

뜻 of or concerned with or related to the future

동 anticipated, planned, expected, awaited, potential

예 *prospective earnings*

---

block [blák]　　　　　　　　　　　*vt.* 막다

뜻 stop from happening or developing

동 bar, hinder, embarrass, blockade, obstruct

예 *They blocked his election.*

levy [lévi]　　　　　　　　　　　　　　　　　　　　　*vt.* 징수하다

图 impose and collect

图 impose, raise, charge, tax, assess

예 *The police levys a large fine.*

---

segregation [sègrigéiʃən]　　　　　　　　　　　　*n.* 분리, 격리

图 separation from others

图 isolation, separation, detachment, seclusion, insulation

예 *segregation of the jury*

---

bulk [bʌlk]　　　　　　　　　　　　　　　　　　*n.* 부피, 용적, 크기

图 the property of something that is great in magnitude

图 mass, size, largeness, magnitude, volume

예 *It is cheaper to buy it in bulk.*

---

consulation [kànsəltéiʃən]　　　　　　　　　　　*n.* 상담, 상의

图 the act of referring or consulting

图 advice, counsel, deliberation, reference, conference

예 *Consultation to an encyclopedia produced the answer.*

---

consult [kənsʌlt]　　　　　　　　　　　　　　　*vt.* 상의하다

图 get or ask advice from

图 ask, confer, advise, interrogate, confabulate

예 *Consult your local broker.*

---

trial [tràiəl]　　　　　　　　　　　　　　　　　*n.* 시도, 시험

图 the act of testing something

图 proof, examination, try, probation, test

예 *He called each flip of the coin a new trial.*

comparable [kámpərəbl]　　　　　　　　　　　　　　*a.* 유사한

围 conforming in every respect

圄 analogous, similar, consonant, corresponding, undifferenced

예 *My sister and I are comparable in appearance.*

compromise [kámprəmaiz]　　　　　　　　　　　　*vi.* 타협하다

围 make concession for conciliation and peace

圄 adjust, negotiate, conciliate, settle, concede

예 *Since nobody will get everything he wants, we all must compromise.*

picnic [píknik]　　　　　　　　　　　　　　　　　*n.* 소풍

围 a day devoted to an outdoor social gathering

圄 outing, excursion, tour, jaunt, trip

예 *We will go on a picnic to the park.*

domestic [dəmestik]　　　　　　　　　　　　*a.* 국내의, 자국의

围 of concern to or concerning the internal affairs of a nation

圄 national, indigenous, municipal, inland, native

예 *Tax rate and highway construction is domestic issues.*

quality [kwáləti]　　　　　　　　　　　　　　　*n.* 가치, 질

围 a degree or grade of excellence or worth

圄 merit, grade, property, attribute, class

예 *The quality of students has risen.*

suspicion [səspíʃən]　　　　　　　　　　　　　*n.* 혐의, 의심

围 doubt about someone's honesty

圄 doubt, mistrust, misgiving, skepticism, distrust

예 *He is clear from suspicion.*

saloon [səlúːn]

🔲 n. 유흥장

医 a room or establishment where alcoholic drinks are served over a counter

동 bar, parlor, ginmill, barroom, taproom

예 *He drowned his sorrows in whiskey at the saloon.*

implication [ìmplikéiʃən]

🔲 n. 함축, 내포

医 something that is inferred (deduced or entailed or implied)

동 indication, denotation, connotation, entailment, innuendo

예 *His resignation had political implications.*

*Vocabulary/Expressions

fascinating [fǽsənèitiŋ]　　　　　　　　　　　　　　　*a.* 매혹적인
- 图 capturing interest as if by a spell
- 图 glamorous, captivating, enchanting, charming, ravishing
- 예 *a fascinating woman*

---

innate [ineit]　　　　　　　　　　　　　　　　　　　*a.* 타고난
- 图 being talented through inherited qualities
- 图 inherent, congenital, inbred, connate, inborn
- 예 *an innate musician*

---

negotiate [nigóuʃièit]　　　　　　　　　　　　　　*vt.* 협상하다
- 图 discuss the terms of an arrangement
- 图 bargain, parley, deal, transact, discuss
- 예 *They negotiated the sale of the house.*

---

chore [tʃɔːr]　　　　　　　　　　　　　　　　　*n.* 자질구레한 일
- 图 a specific piece of work required to be done as a duty or for a specific fee
- 图 labor, sweat, toil, burden, housework, task, travail
- 예 *The chore of repairing the engine took several hours.*

---

enter [éntər]　　　　　　　　　　　　　　　　　*vt.* ~에 들어가다
- 图 come or go into
- 图 insert, access, invade, penetrate, infiltrate
- 예 *The boat entered an area of shallow marshes.*

---

accommodate [əkámədeit]　　　　　　　　　　　　*vt.* 수용하다
- 图 hold without crowding
- 图 contain, receive, admit, fit, hold, house, take in
- 예 *This hotel can accommodate 250 guests.*

hang [hǽŋ]   *vi.* 걸리다, 매달리다

- 뜻 be suspended or hanging
- 동 adhere, suspend, hold, swing, dangle
- 예 *The flag hung on the wall.*

addictive [ədíktiv]   *a.* 중독성의

- 뜻 causing or characterized by addiction
- 동 habit-forming, devoted, hooking, enslaving, obsessive
- 예 *addictive behavior*

supervision [sù:pərvíʒən]   *n.* 감독

- 뜻 management by overseeing the performance or operation of a person or group
- 동 control, observation, inspection, surveillance, oversight
- 예 *I have supervision over the test.*

inheritance [inhérətəns]   *n.* 상속재산

- 뜻 any attribute or immaterial possession that is inherited from ancestors
- 동 heritance, bequest, heritage, patrimony, legacy
- 예 *My only inheritance was my mother's blessing.*

bleak [blíːk]   *a.* 황량한

- 뜻 offering little or no hope
- 동 dreary, desolate, dismal, gloomy, black
- 예 *The future looked bleak.*

deduct [didʌkt]   *vt.* 빼다

- 뜻 make a subtraction
- 동 lessen, curtail, discount, subtract, abate
- 예 *Deduct this amount from my paycheck.*

torrent [tɔːrənt]
n. 연발

圄 an overwhelming number or amount

同 flood, flow, deluge, spate, inundation

예 *a torrent of requests*

---

innocent [ínəsənt]
a. 순진한

圄 lacking in sophistication or worldliness

同 sincere, naive, pure, unsophisticated, ingenuous

예 *a child's innocent stare*

---

synthetic [sinθetik]
a. 인조의

圄 not of natural origin

同 artificial, manufactured, unnatural, factitious, semisynthetic

예 *synthetic leather*

---

figure [fígjər]
vt. 상상하다, 마음에 그리다

圄 see in one's mind

同 picture, envision, image, visualize, see

예 *I can figure a risk in this strategy.*

---

tenant [tenənt]
n. 차용자; 거주자

圄 someone who pays rent to use land or a building or a car that is owned by someone else

同 inhabitant, dweller, occupant, leaseholder, renter, resident

예 *The landlord can evict a tenant who doesn't pay the rent.*

---

chilly [tʃíli]
a. 차가운

圄 lacking warmth of feeling

同 icy, cool, wintry, frigid, bleak

예 *a chilly greeting*

fluctuate [flʌktʃueit]　　　　　　　　　　*vi.* 동요하다, 흔들리다

图 be unstable

图 vibrate, go up and down, vacillate, oscillate, waver

예 *The stock market fluctuates.*

exchange [ikstʃeindʒ]　　　　　　　*vt.* 교환하다, 환전하다

图 the act of changing one thing for another thing

图 replace, trade, reciprocate, trade, deal, alternate, substitute

예 *I exchange ideas with him.*

mellow [melou]　　　　　　　　*a.* (과실이) 익은, 달콤한

图 having a full and pleasing flavor through proper aging

图 mature, soft, ripe, softened, mellifluous

예 *The apple is mellow.*

quench [kwéntʃ]　　　　　　　*vt.* (불, 빛 등을) 끄다

图 put out, as of fires, flames, or lights

图 extinguish, douse, slake, put out, suppress

예 *Quench the candles.*

fastidious [fæstidiəs]　　　　　　　　　　*a.* 까다로운

图 giving careful attention to detail

图 meticulous, demanding, captious, finicky, fussy, exacting

예 *She is fastidious about personal cleanliness.*

predictable [pridíktəbl]　　　　　　　*a.* 예언할 수 있는

图 capable of being foretold

图 anticipated, expected, calculable, sure-fire, foreseeable

예 *predictable outcomes*

nutritious [njutríʃəs]　　　　　　　　　　　　　*a.* 영양이 되는
- 图 of or providing nourishment
- 동 alimentary, nourishing, alimental, nutritive
- 예 *good nutritious stew*

paralyze [pǽrəlàiz]　　　　　　　　　　　　　*vt.* 무능하게 만들다
- 图 make powerless and unable to function
- 동 immobilize, stupefy, stun, freeze, numb
- 예 *Fear paralyzed her.*

output [àutpùt]　　　　　　　　　　　　　　　*n.* 생산
- 图 production of a certain amount
- 동 production, yield, performance, achievement
- 예 *annual output*

affective [əféktiv]　　　　　　　　　　　　　*a.* 감정적인
- 图 characterized by emotion
- 동 affectional, stirring, emotional, touching
- 예 *affective disorder*

stir [stə́:r]　　　　　　　　　　　　　　　　　*vt.* 휘젓다
- 图 move an implement through
- 동 mix, shake, agitate, move, budge
- 예 *Stirring the soup is very important proceed.*

fake [féik]　　　　　　　　　　　　　　　　　*vt.* 속이다
- 图 tamper, with the purpose of deception
- 동 pretend, disguise, feign, forge, put on, falsify
- 예 *He likes to fake me.*

casualty [kǽʒuəlti]　　　　　　　　　　　　　　　　　　　*n.* 피해자

뜻 someone injured or killed or captured or missing in a military engagement

동 scapegoat, injured, wounded, prey, victim, killed

예 *heavy casualties*

---

chronic [kránik]　　　　　　　　　　　　　　　　　　　*a.* 만성적인

뜻 being long-lasting and recurrent or characterized by long suffering

동 incessant, continuing, recurrent, inveterate, confirmed

예 *chronic indigestion*

---

keen [kíːn]　　　　　　　　　　　　　　　　　　　*a.* 날카로운

뜻 intense or sharp

동 sharp, acute, incisive, piercing, trenchant

예 *I suffered keen pain.*

---

research [risə́ːrtʃ]　　　　　　　　　　　　　　　　　*vi.* 조사하다

뜻 inquire into

동 investigate, examine, inquire, explore, search

예 *He researched for information on his relatives on the web.*

---

entertainment [èntərtéinmənt]　　　　　　　　　　　*n.* 오락, 연예

뜻 an activity that is diverting and that holds the attention

동 amusement, recreation, pastime, diversion, fun

예 *a musical entertainment*

---

rummage [rʌmidʒ]　　　　　　　　　　　　　　　　*vi.* 뒤지며 찾다

뜻 search haphazardly

동 seek, search, ransack, investigate, examine

예 *We rummaged through the drawers.*

confidence [kánfədəns]　　　　　　　　　　　　　　　*n.* 신임

- 图 freedom from doubt
- 동 faith, belief, trust, reliance, assurance
- 예 *After that failure he lost his confidence.*

---

victim [víktim]　　　　　　　　　　　　　　　　　　*n.* 희생자

- 图 a person who is tricked or swindled
- 동 casualty, scapegoat, sacrifice, sufferer, martyr
- 예 *He's the victim of the Korean war in 1950.*

---

acute [əkjú:t]　　　　　　　　　　　　　　　　　　*a.* 격렬한

- 图 extremely sharp or intense
- 동 severe, penetrating, keen, piercing, sharp
- 예 *She felt acute annoyance.*

---

voting [vóutiŋ]　　　　　　　　　　　　　　　　*n.* 투표, 선거

- 图 a choice that is made by counting the number of people in favor of each alternative
- 동 ballot, polling, choosing, deciding
- 예 *They allowed just one voting per person.*

---

predict [pridíkt]　　　　　　　　　　　　　　　*vt.* 예언하다

- 图 tell or declaire beforehand
- 동 foretell, anticipate, presage, forebode, prognosticate
- 예 *She predicted the outcome of the election.*

---

allegedly [əlédʒidli]　　　　　　　　　　*adv.* 전해진 바에 의하면

- 图 according to what has been alleged
- 동 assertedly, supposedly, purportedly, professedly, avowedly
- 예 *He was on trial for allegedly murdering his wife.*

pluck [plʌk]　　　　　　　　　　　　　　　　　　*vt.* 잡아뜯다

圐 pull or pull out sharply

통 pull, grab, tweak, gather, pick

예 *Don't pluck the flowers off the bush.*

---

guilty [gílti]　　　　　　　　　　　　　　　　　　*a.* 유죄의

圐 responsible for or chargeable with a reprehensible act

통 blameworthy, condemned, delinquent, sinful, peccant, culpable

예 *That man is guilty of murder.*

---

convenience [kənvíːnjəns]　　　　　　　　　　　*n.* 편의, 편리

圐 the quality of being useful and convenient

통 ease, fitness, comfort, suitability, accommodation

예 *They offered the convenience of an installment plan.*

---

gratify [grǽtəfài]　　　　　　　　　　　　　　　*vt.* 만족시키다

圐 make happy or satisfied

통 satisfy, please, enchant, content, appease

예 *Teacher gratifies my curiosity.*

---

optical [áptikəl]　　　　　　　　　　　　　　　　*a.* 눈의

圐 relating to or using sight

통 optic, visual, visible, discernible, ocular

예 *an optical illusion*

---

exhibition [eksəbiʃən]　　　　　　　　　　　　　*n.* 전시

圐 the act of exhibiting

통 exposition, display, demonstration, showing

예 *a remarkable exhibition of musicianship*

---

subscribe [səbskràib]　　　　　　　　　　　　　　vt. 기부하다

图 pay an amount of money as a contribution to a charity or service

통 donate, support, contribute, grant, consent, pledge

예 *I subscribed $10 a month to my favorite radio station.*

demonstrate [deménstreit]　　　　　　　　　　　vt. 증명하다

图 provide evidence for

통 certify, attest, prove, evince, manifest

예 *This decision demonstrates his sense of fairness.*

*Vocabulary/Expressions

complexion [kəmplékʃən]　　　　　　　　　　　　　　*n.* 안색, 혈색
- 医 the coloring of a person's face
- 同 skin color, flush, hue, tint, skin tone
- 예 *a dark complexion*

exceed [iksi:d]　　　　　　　　　　　　　　　　　*vt.* ~의 한도를 넘다
- 医 be or do something to a greater degree
- 同 transcend, excel, surpass, outdo, transgress
- 예 *This exceeds all my expectations.*

appointed [əpɔintid]　　　　　　　　　　　　　*a.* 정해진, 약속된
- 医 fixed or established especially by order or command
- 同 decreed, ordained, prescribed, nominated, determined
- 예 *Please, do your appointed task.*

conservation [kànsərveiʃən]　　　　　　　　　　*n.* 보존, 유지
- 医 an occurrence of improvement by virtue of preventing loss or injury or other change
- 同 preservation, keeping, conservancy, maintenance, protection
- 예 *conservation area*

insolvent [insálvənt]　　　　　　　　　　　　　*a.* 지불 불능한
- 医 unable to meet or discharge financial obligations
- 同 bankrupt, unbalanced, undone, indebted, strapped
- 예 *an insolvent person*

connection [kənekʃən]　　　　　　　　　　　　　*n.* 관계, 관련
- 医 a relation between things or event
- 同 contact, association, reciporcity, relation, ally
- 예 *There was a connection between eating that pickle and having that nightmare.*

desolation [dèsəléiʃən]
n. 쓸쓸함, 처량함

图 sadness resulting from being forsaken or abandoned

图 forlornness, loneliness, unhappiness, sorrow, mourning

예 *My desolations are determined.*

deformity [difɔ́:rməti]
n. 기형

图 an appearance that has been spoiled or is misshapen

图 disfigurement, contortion, misshapenness, distortion, malformation

예 *She is suffering from facial deformity.*

advertising [ǽdvərtàiziŋ]
n. 광고

图 a public promotion of some product or service

图 announcement, proclamation, publicity, hoopla

예 *advertising agency*

constitute [kánstətjuːt]
vt. 구성하다

图 form or compose

图 compose, form, establish, comprise, institute

예 *These constitute my entire belonging.*

seasoning [síːzəniŋ]
n. 간맞춤, 조미료

图 something added to food primarily for the savor it imparts

图 flavorer, seasoner, condiment, flavoring, relish

예 *The chef tastes for seasoning.*

conserve [kənsə́:rv]
vt. 보존하다, 유지하다

图 keep in safety and protect from harm, decay, loss, or destruction

图 save, preserve, keep up, maintain, retain

예 *Children must be taught to conserve our national heritage.*

deter [ditə́ːr] *vt.* 단념시키다

图 try to prevent

图 dissuade, restrain, obstruct, discourage, obviate

例 *Negative campaigning will only deter people.*

---

autograph [ɔ́ːtəgræf] *vt.* 서명하다

图 mark with one's signature

图 sign, endorse, inscribe, handwrite, subscribe

例 *The author autographed his book.*

---

pinpoint [pínpɔint] *vt.* ~의 위치를 정확하게 나타내다

图 locate exactly

图 diagnose, nail, define, locate, spot

例 *The chemists could not pinpoint the identity of the chromosome.*

---

target [tɑ́ːrgit] *n.* 과녁, 목표

图 the goal intended to be attained

图 mark, aim, object, goal, purpose

例 *The sole target of her trip was to see her children.*

---

behemoth [bihíːməθ] *n.* 거인, 거대한 것

图 someone or something that is abnormally large and powerful

图 giant, goliath, monster, huge, mammoth, monster

例 *a land of behemoths*

---

overtly [ouvə́ːrtli] *adv.* 명백히, 공공연하게

图 in an overt manner

图 readily, avowedly, publicly, willingly, openly

例 *He did it overtly.*

thrift [θríft]

n. 절약, 검약

- 뜻 reluctance to spend money unnecessarily
- 동 austerity, parsimony, prudence, stinginess, frugality
- 예 *He always practices thrift.*

musty [mʌsti]

a. 곰팡내나는

- 뜻 covered with or smelling of mold
- 동 spoiled, moldy, faded, malodorous, stinking
- 예 *musty bread*

turbulence [tə́:rbjuləns]

n. 소란, 불온

- 뜻 a state of violent disturbance and disorder
- 동 upheaval, disorder, agitation, turmoil, confusion
- 예 *The industrial revolution was a period of great turbulence.*

alien [éiljən]

a. 이질적인

- 뜻 not contained in or deriving from the essential nature of something
- 동 foreign, inappropriate, contrary, extrinsic, incongruous
- 예 *Jealousy is alien to her nature.*

crime [kràim]

n. 죄

- 뜻 usually considered an evil act
- 동 sin, guilt, felony, offence, misdeed
- 예 *a long record of crimes*

eloquent [éləkwənt]

a. 웅변의, 능변인

- 뜻 expressing yourself readily, clearly, effectively
- 동 fluent, facile, articulate, well-expressed, silver-tongued
- 예 *eloquent speech*

adopt [ədápt] *vt.* 채택하다

医 take on a certain form, attribute, or aspect

동 accept, embrace, acquire, take, espouse, assent

예 *He adopted an air of superiority.*

epidemic [èpədémik] *a.* 유행성의

医 attacking or affecting many individuals in a community or a population simultaneously

동 widespread, catching, infectious, contagious, prevalent

예 *an epidemic outbreak of influenza*

enforce [infɔ́:rs] *vt.* 실시하다, 집행하다

医 ensure observance of laws and rules

동 compel, accomplish, begin, apply, impose

예 *Enforce the rules to everyone.*

conviction [kənvíkʃən] *n.* 확신

医 an unshakable belief in something without need for proof or evidence

동 opinion, belief, faith, confidence, persuasion

예 *a conviction about the news*

guarantee [gæ̀rəntí:] *vt.* 보증하다

医 give surety or assume responibility

동 secure, assure, confirm, warrant, promise

예 *I guarantee this information.*

authenticity [ɔ̀:θentísəti] *n.* 확실성, 진실성

医 undisputed credibility

동 genuineness, veritableness, legitimacy, accuracy

예 *authenticity of his work*

proximity [prɑksiməti] *n.* 근접

图 the property of being close together

图 adjacency, nearness, closeness, vicinity, propinquity

예 *The proximity of the apartments to a school of high makes its payment very expensive.*

---

interruption [ìntərʌpʃən] *n.* 중단, 방해

图 a breach or break, caused by the abrupt interevention of something foreign

图 interferance, cessation, disturbance, pause, stoppage, hindrance

예 *The telephone is an annoying interruption.*

---

constant [kάnstənt] *a.* 불변의

图 uninterrupted in time and indefinitely long continuing

图 unceasing, ceaseless, perpetual, incessant, unremitting

예 *the constant search for happiness*

---

arena [ərí:nə] *n.* 활동무대

图 a particular environment or walk of life

图 sphere, domain, area, orbit, field

예 *His social arena is limited.*

---

simmer [símər] *vt.* 부글부글 끓이다

图 boil slowly at low temperature

图 boil, seethe, parboil, stew, warm

예 *Simmer the water gently for 5 minutes.*

---

trustee [trʌsti:] *n.* 보관인

图 a person to whom legal title to property is entrusted to use for another's benefit

图 custodian, administrator, guardian, curator, fiduciary

예 *a trustee in bankruptcy*

---

recline [riklàin]   *vi.* 기대다

㊑ lean in a comfortable resting position

㊀ lean, stretch, lie down, lounge, repose, slant

㊊ *He was reclining on the couch.*

---

ecosystem [ekousistəm]   *n.* 생태계

㊑ a system formed by the interaction of a community of organisms with their physical environment

㊀ ecological community

㊊ *closed ecosystem*

---

shipment [ʃipmənt]   *n.* 선적, 수송

㊑ goods carried by a large vehicle

㊀ lading, cargo, load, freight, loading

㊊ *Where does the shipment to be sent?*

---

inquisitive [inkwízətiv]   *a.* 탐구적인

㊑ inquiring or appearing to inquire

㊀ curious, analytical, speculative, questioning, wondering, investigative

㊊ *an inquiring look*

---

costume [kástju:m]   *n.* 복장

㊑ the attire worn in a play or at a fancy dress ball

㊀ apparel, robes, getup, clothing, dress

㊊ *He won the prize for best costume.*

---

collateral [kəlǽtərəl]   *a.* 부대적인

㊑ serving to support or corroborate

㊀ accessory, secondary, accompany, substantiative, added, subordinate

㊊ *collateral evidence*

Day 20

inverse [invə́:rs]   *a.* 반대의
图 opposite in nature or effect or relation to another quantity
동 opposite, contrary, inverted, reverse, converse
예 *inverse function*

apparent [əpǽrənt]   *a.* 명백한
图 clearly revealed to the mind or the senses or judgment
동 evident, plain, clear, unmistakable, manifest
예 *The effects of the drought are apparent to anyone who sees the parched fields.*

wreck [rék]   *vt.* 엉망으로 파괴하다
图 smash or break forcefully
동 ruin, destroy, subvert, devastate, smash
예 *The kid wrecked the car.*

standard [stǽndərd]   *n.* 표준, 기준
图 a basis for comparison
동 norm, criterion, measure, guideline, touchstone
예 *The schools comply with federal standards.*

pollution [pəlú:ʃən]   *n.* 오염
图 the act of contaminating or polluting
동 dirtiness, contamination, taint, defilement, uncleanness
예 *environmental pollution*

dependable [dipendəbl]   *a.* 믿을 수 있는
图 worthy of reliance or trust
동 trustworthy, certain, responsible, reliable, safe
예 *a dependable worker*

encourage [inkə́:ridʒ] vt. 격려하다

囡 spur on

图 enegize, hearten, promote, cheer, stimulate, exhilarate

例 *His financial success encouraged him to look for a wife.*

stand [stǽnd] vt. 견디다

囡 put up with something or somebody unpleasant

图 endure, bear, tolerate, stay, abide

例 *I cannot stand his constant criticism anymore.*

*Vocabulary/Expressions

---

fertile [fə́:rtl]
a. 비옥한

图 marked by great fruitfulness

图 fruitful, productive, rich, flourishing, thriving, abundant

예 *fertile farmland*

---

comment [kάment]
n. 논평, 비평

图 a statement that expresses a personal opinion or belief or adds information

图 remark, criticism, mention, commentary, dictum

예 *From time to time, she contributed a personal comment on his account.*

---

incumbent [inkʌmbənt]
a. 현직의

图 currently holding an office

图 official, current, present

예 *the incumbent governor*

---

overseas [óuvərsí:z]
a. 해외의

图 in a foreign country

图 abroad, exotic, foreign, extraneous, external

예 *overseas markets*

---

occupant [άkjupənt]
n. 점유자

图 someone who lives at a particular place for a prolonged period or who was born there

图 holder, dweller, resident, occupier, tenant

예 *an occupant of a house*

---

squander [skwάndər]
vt. 낭비하다

图 spend extravagantly

图 waste, blow, consume, dissipate, lavish

예 *You squandered the opportunity to get and advanced degree.*

---

dismiss [dismís]   *vt.* 해고하다

图 discharge from an office or position

图 displace, lay off, turn off, fire, terminate

예 *The boss dismissed his secretary today.*

---

essentially [isénʃəli]   *adv.* 본질적으로

图 in essence, at botton or by one's (or its) very nature

图 basically, virtually, fundamentally, necessarily, actually

예 *He is essentially dishonest.*

---

prevention [privénʃən]   *n.* 예방

图 stopping from doing something or being in a certain state

图 avoidance, obstruction, thwarting, blockage, impediment

예 *Many was allocated to study the cause and prevention of influenza.*

---

intensive [inténsiv]   *a.* 격렬한

图 characterized by a high degree or intensity

图 intense, hard, severe, profound, concentrated

예 *intensive conditions*

---

rip [ríp]   *vi.* 찢어지다

图 be torn violently

图 tear, cut, rend, rive, pull

예 *The curtain ripped from top to bottom.*

---

accountant [əkáuntənt]   *n.* 회계원

图 someone who maintains and audits business accounts

图 actuary, bookkeeper, controller, calculator, CPA

예 public accountant

---

aggressive [əgrésiv]
a. 공격적인

图 characteristic of an enemy or one eager to fight

图 offensive, belligerent, hostile, contentious, disruptive

예 *He is an aggressive driver.*

grant [grǽnt]
vt. 주다

图 give as judged due or on the basis of merit

图 give, award, confer, bestow, concede

예 *The referee granted a free kick to the team.*

degrade [digréid]
vt. 품위를 떨어뜨리다

图 reduce in worth or character, usually verbally

图 shame, humiliate, demean, put down, disgrace

예 *She tends to degrade younger women colleagues.*

tariff [tǽrif]
n. 관세

图 a government tax on imports or exports

图 duty, assessment, tax, impost, toll, customs

예 *revenue tariff*

sensitive [sénsətiv]
a. 민감한

图 responsive to physical stimuli

图 susceptible, touchy, delicate, tender, impressionable

예 *sensitive skin*

vacant [véikənt]
a. 빈자리의

图 without an occupant or incumbent

图 empty, unoccupied, available, unengaged

예 *The throne is never vacant.*

insurmountable [ìnsərmàuntəbl]　　　　*a.* 능가할 수 없는, 이겨내기 어려운

图 not capable of being surmounted or overcome

图 unconquerable, unsurmountable, impossible, impregnable

예 *insurmountable disadvantages*

insatiable [inséiʃəbl]　　　　*a.* 만족할 줄 모르는, 탐욕스러운

图 impossible to satisfy

图 gready, voracious, insatiate, rapacious, demanding

예 *He has an insatiable demand for old buildings to restore.*

respond [rispánd]　　　　*vt.* 대답하다

图 react verbally

图 reply, react, answer, rejoin, return

예 *We responded that we would accept the invitation.*

veil [véil]　　　　*vt.* 감추다, 숨기다

图 make undecipherable or imperceptible by obscuring or concealing

图 obscure, blot out, hide, disguise, enfold

예 *He veiled her to survive.*

edit [édit]　　　　*vt.* 편집하다

图 prepare for publication or presentation by correcting, revising, or adapting

图 redact, correct, rewrite, alter, refine

예 *Edit a book on lexical semantics.*

unanimous [ju:nǽnəməs]　　　　*a.* 만장일치의, 합의의

图 in complete agreement

图 concerted, harmonious, accepted, united, homogenous

예 *an unanimous decision*

conveyance [kənvéiəns]
n. 운반, 수송

图 the act of moving something from one location to another

图 transportation, carriage, movement, transference

예 *a public conveyance*

---

irritable [írətəbl]
a. 화를 잘내는

图 very susceptible of anger or passion

图 bad-tempered, crabby, testy, complaining, touchy

예 *an incorrigibly irritable young man*

---

leaflet [li:flit]
n. 광고전단

图 a small book usually having a paper cover

图 handbill, booklet, folder, brochure, pamphlet

예 *Distributing leaflets is not easy.*

---

travel [trǽvəl]
vi. 여행하다

图 undertake a journey or trip.

图 journey, voyage, tour, jaunt, peregrinate

예 *Many people like to travel abroad.*

---

operate [ápəreit]
vi. 작용하다

图 perform as expected when applied

图 act, go, function, run, work

예 *The washing machine won't operate unless it's plugged in.*

---

witty [wíti]
a. 재치있는

图 combining clever conception and facetious expression

图 funny, clever, amusing, epigrammatic, ingenious

예 *His sermons were unpredictably witty and satirical as well as eloquent.*

profit [práfit]   *n.* 이익, 이득, 흑자, 이윤

图 the excess of revenues over outlays in a given period of time

图 earnings, income, benefit, emoluments, interest

例 *He managed to multiply his profits.*

---

application [æ̀pləkéiʃən]   *n.* 적용, 사용

图 using something for a particular purpose

图 operation, use, function, practice, utilization

例 *The doctor prescribed a topical application of iodine.*

---

single [síŋgl]   *a.* 단 하나의

图 existing alone or consisting of one entity or part or aspect or individual

图 sole, only, singular, one, solitary

例 *a single survivor*

---

department [dipá:rtmənt]   *n.* 부서

图 a specialized division of a large organization

图 section, bureau, division, agency, unit

例 *She got a job in the historical department of the Treasury.*

---

election [ilékʃən]   *n.* 선거

图 a vote to select the winner of a position or political office

图 selection, balloting, poll, choosing, voting

例 *The results of the election will be announced tonight.*

---

slack [slǽk]   *vi.* 침체하다, 약해지다

图 a noticeable deterioration in performance or quality

图 slump, drop-off, sluggish, falling off

例 *The stock market is slacking.*

---

shabby [ʃǽbi]   *a.* 허름한

뜻 showing signs of wear and tear

동 broken-down, decrepit, ratty, dilapidated, faded

예 *shabby furniture*

---

auditorium [ɔ̀ːdətɔ́ːriəm]   *n.* 강당

뜻 the area of a theater or concert hall where the audience sits

동 hall, arena, playhouse, hippodrome, amphitheater

예 *an auditorium with seating accommodation for one thousand*

---

decline [diklain]   *vt.* 거절하다

뜻 refuse to accept

동 reject, reprobate, deny, refuse, repudiate

예 *He declined my offer of hospitality.*

---

normal [nɔ́ːrməl]   *a.* 표준의; 보통의

뜻 conforming with or constituting a norm or standard or level or type or social
norm

동 standard, rational, reasonable, sound, right

예 *normal diplomatic relations*

---

available [əvéiləbl]   *a.* 이용할 수 있는

뜻 obtainable or accessible and ready for use or service

동 accessible, disposable, applicable, obtainable, serviceable

예 *Overnight accommodations are available.*

---

preference [prefərəns]   *n.* 더 좋아함

뜻 a predisposition in favor of something

동 predilection, inclination, favoritism, predisposition

예 *a preference for expensive cars*

rely [rilài] *vi.* 의지하다

圐 have confidence or faith in

圐 lean, depend, trust, swear, confide

圐 *Rely on your friends.*

disaster [dizǽstər] *n.* 재앙

圐 a state of extreme ruin and misfortune

圐 misfortune, calamity, affliction, evil, mishap

圐 *His policies were a disaster.*

equipment [ikwípmənt] *n.* 장비, 비품

圐 an instrumentality needed for an undertaking or to perform a service

圐 kit, apparatus, gear, devices, tackle

圐 *audiovisual equipment*

conspirator [kənspírətər] *n.* 공모자

圐 a member of a combination of p eople for an evil purpose

圐 accomplice, collaborator, plotter, connive, machinator

圐 *He executed all the conspirators who attempted a rebellion.*

outlaw [àutlɔ:] *vt.* 금지하다

圐 declare illegal

圐 forbid, illegalize, prohibit, proscribe, criminalize

圐 *Marijuana is outlawed in the U.S.*

representative [reprizentətiv] *n.* 대표자

圐 a person who is a delegate or spokesperson for others

圐 delegate, deputy, agent, exponent, proxy

圐 *The representative of conference works well.*

appropriate [əprouprieit] *a.* 적당한

뜻 suitable for a particular person or place or condition etc

동 proper, fit, relevant, opportune, felicitous, congruous, apt

예 *This book is not appropriate for children.*

indifferent [indifərənt] *a.* 무관심한

뜻 marked by a lack of interest

동 apathetic, unconcerned, disinterested, nonchalant

예 *an indifferent audience*

*Vocabulary/Expressions

sour [sàuər]
_a._ 심술궂은

㊂ showing a brooding ill humor

㊂ dour, morose, glum, moody, sullen

㊂ _a sour temper_

---

competitive [kəmpetətiv]
_a._ 경쟁의

㊂ involving competition or competitiveness

㊂ rival, emulous, competing, vying, opposing

㊂ _competitive games_

---

onset [á:nsèt]
_n._ 습격, 공격

㊂ an offensive against an enemy

㊂ attack, onset, assault, strike, onrush

㊂ _The onset began at dawn._

---

institution [ìnstətjúːʃən]
_n._ 설립, 창립

㊂ the act of starting something for the first time

㊂ initiation, foundation, origination, creation, instauration

㊂ _the institution of a new scientific society_

---

apparent [əpǽrənt]
_a._ 명백한

㊂ clearly revealed to the mind or the senses or judgment

㊂ evident, plain, clear, unmistakable, manifest

㊂ _The effects of the drought are apparent to anyone who sees the parched fields._

---

announcement [ənaunsmənt]
_n._ 공고, 고시, 고지

㊂ a formal public statement

㊂ declaration, proclamation, annunciation, bulletin, notification

㊂ _The government made an announcement about changes in the drug war._

outlay [àutlèi]   *n.* 지출, 소비

图 the act of spending or disbursing money

图 expenditure, spending, disbursement, disbursal, expenses

예 *cash outlay*

---

humanity [hju:mǽnəti]   *n.* 인류

图 all of the living human inhabitants of the earth

图 mankind, people, humanness, humankind, society

예 *All the humanity loves a lover.*

---

avid [ǽvid]   *a.* 욕심많은

图 ardently or excessively desirous

图 eager, greedy, esurient, grasping, rapacious

예 *I am avid for adventure.*

---

transplant [trænsplǽnt]   *vt.* 이주시키다

图 transfer from one place or period to another

图 transfer, immigrate, resettle, transpose, relocate

예 *The ancient Greek story was transplanted into Modern America.*

---

bounce [bauns]   *vi.* 튀다

图 spring back

图 bound, rebound, recoil, resile, reverberate

예 *The rubber ball bounced.*

---

asset [ǽset]   *n.* 자산

图 a useful or valuable quality

图 plus, credit, resource, benefit, advantage

예 *working asset*

---

compound [kámpaund]　　　　　　　　　　　　　　　　*vt.* 혼합하다

图 put or add together

图 mix, combine, amalgamate, concoct, mingle

예 *He compounds resources to make fuel.*

---

devour [diváuər]　　　　　　　　　　　　　　　　*vt.* 게걸스레 먹다

图 eat greedily

图 guttle, consume, swallow, imbibe, relish

예 *He devoured three sandwiches.*

---

content [kántent]　　　　　　　　　　　　　　　　*n.* 내용

图 everything that is included in a collection and that is held or included in something

图 matter, essence, substance, meaning, idea

예 *He emptied the contents of his pockets.*

---

hoard [hɔ:rd]　　　　　　　　　　　　　　　　*vt.* 저장하다, 축적하다

图 get or gather together

图 collect, accumulate, pile up, amass, compile

예 *She is hoarding a lot of data for her thesis.*

---

vital [váitl]　　　　　　　　　　　　　　　　*a.* 극히 중대한

图 urgently needed

图 essential, cardinal, indispensable, critical, prerequisite

예 *a vital element of the plan*

---

threaten [θrétn]　　　　　　　　　　　　　　　　*vt.* 위협하다

图 present a danger to

图 endanger, menace, threaten, jeopardize, imperil

예 *The pollution is threatening the crops.*

---

outcast [àutkæst]   *n.* 부랑자

뜻 a person who is excluded from a society

동 castaway, derelict, exile, tramp, bum

예 *social outcast*

---

scrupulous [skrúːpjuləs]   *a.* 꼼꼼한

뜻 characterized by extreme care and great effort

동 punctilious, conscientious, painstaking, punctual, rigorous

예 *They admired his scrupulous professional integrity.*

---

integration [ìntəgréiʃən]   *n.* 통합

뜻 the act of combining into an integral whole

동 consolidation, unification, amalgamation, union, mixture

예 *an integration of two corporations*

---

achievement [ətʃíːvmənt]   *n.* 달성

뜻 the action of accomplishing something

동 success, accomplishment, performance, attainment, fulfilment

예 *achievement test*

---

toss [tɔːs, tás]   *vt.* 던지다

뜻 throw with a light motion

동 flip, pitch, cast, fling, peg

예 *Toss me the newspaper.*

---

rule [rúːl]   *n.* 규칙

뜻 a principle or condition that customarily governs behavior

동 principle, standard, law, precept, norm, regulation

예 *Short haircuts were the rule of my middle school.*

---

artisan [ɑ́:rtəzən]   *n.* 장인

圐 a skilled worker who practices some trade or handicraft

동 master, professional, craftsman, journeyman, builder

예 *skilled artisan*

---

enact [inǽkt]   *vt.* 규정하다, 제정하다

圐 order by virtue of superior authority

동 authorize, legislate, establish, appoint, execute, proclaim, constitute

예 *The Parliament enacted and administered the law in 1985.*

---

apathy [ǽpəθi]   *n.* 냉담, 무관심

圐 the trait of lacking enthusiasm for or interest in things generally

동 indifference, disregard, numbness, disinterest, lethargy

예 *She has an apathy to him.*

---

opening [oupəniŋ]   *n.* 틈

圐 an open or empty space in or between things

동 crack, gap, hole, space, aperture

예 *There was a small opening between the trees.*

---

suspicious [səspíʃəs]   *a.* 의심하는

圐 openly distrustful and unwilling to confide

동 distrustful, incredulous, leery, cautious, skeptical, questioning

예 *suspicious behavior*

---

fallible [fǽləbl]   *a.* 오류에 빠지기 쉬운

圐 likely to fail or make errors

동 errable, careless, heedless, imperfect, faulty

예 *Everyone is fallible to some degree.*

---

throb [θráb]　　　　　　　　　　　　　　　　　　　　*vi.* 고동치다

뜻 pulsate or pound with abnormal force

동 pulsate, beat, pound, flutter, resonate, twitter

예 *Her heart was throbbing.*

---

inevitability [inèvətəbíləti]　　　　　　　　　　　*n.* 불가피함, 필연성

뜻 the quality of being unavoidable

동 predestination, necessity, certainty, ineluctability, karma

예 *inevitability of globalization*

---

range [reindʒ]　　　　　　　　　　　　　　　　　　*vt.* 정렬시키다

뜻 lay out orderly or logically in a line or as if in a line

동 classify, align, line, order, categorize

예 *Range the clothes on your own, please.*

---

agency [eidʒənsi]　　　　　　　　　　　　　　　　*n.* 대리, 대행

뜻 the state of serving as an official and authorized delegate or agent

동 intervention, medium, organization, bureau, department, firm

예 *advertising agency*

---

revolutionary [rèvəlú:ʃənèri]　　　　　　　　　　*a.* 혁명의

뜻 markedly new or introducing radical change

동 radical, progressive, innovative, developing, advancing

예 *a revolutionary discovery*

---

transfer [trænsfə́:r]　　　　　　　　　　　　　*vt.* 옮기다, 나르다, 건네다

뜻 move from one place to another

동 convey, deliver, shift, displace, carry, relocate, transport

예 *He transfered the data.*

---

emit [imit]　　　　　　　　　　　　　　　　　　　　　*vt.* 방출하다

图 give off, send forth, or discharge as of light, heat, or radiation, vapor, etc.

동 radiate, issue, beam, transmit, shed

예 *The ozone layer blocks some harmful rays which the sun emits.*

---

inquiry [inkwàiəri]　　　　　　　　　　　　　　　　　　*n.* 연구

图 a search for knowledge

동 inspection, survey, enquiry, research, investigation

예 *Their pottery deserves more inquiry than it has received.*

---

graduate [grǽdʒuèit]　　　　　　　　　　　　　　　　*vt.* 졸업시키다

图 confer an academic degree upon

동 take a degree, grant diploma, certify, finish, earn

예 *This school graduates 2,000 students each year.*

---

plastic [plǽstik]　　　　　　　　　　　　　　　　　　　*a.* 가소성의

图 capable of being molded or modeled

동 flexible, soft, pilable, moldable, resilient

예 *plastic substances such as wax or clay*

---

attach [ətǽtʃ]　　　　　　　　　　　　　　　　　　　　*vi.* 붙다

图 stick to, become in contact with

동 adgere, fix, stick, join, tie, add, bind

예 *The spider's thread attached to the window sill.*

---

substantial [səbstǽnʃəl]　　　　　　　　　　　　　*a.* 상당한, 많은

图 fairly large

동 ample, plentiful, abundant, hefty, large

예 *He won by a substantial margin.*

Day 22

innovate [ínəvèit]   *vt.* 도입하다
图 bring something new to an environment
图 create, introduce, conceive, institute, begin
예 *A new word processor was innovated.*

extort [ikstɔ:rt]   *vt.* 강탈하다
图 obtain by coercion or intimidation
图 force, extact, squeeze, blackmail, cheat, wring
예 *They extorted money from the executive by threatening to reveal his past to the company boss.*

labor [leibər]   *n.* 노동
图 productive work
图 work, toil, chore, job, task, undertaking, travail
예 *His labor did not require a great deal of skill.*

abuse [əbjú:s]   *vt.* 오용하다, 악용하다
图 change the inherent purpose or function of something
图 pervert, misuse, violate, corrupt, mishandle, squander
예 *Don't abuse the system.*

throw [θróu]   *vt.* 던지다
图 propel through the air
图 fling, pitch, toss, cast, hurl
예 *The boy throws a Frisbee.*

gimmick [gímik]   *n.* 속임수
图 any clever maneuver
图 trick, device, stratagem, ruse, wile, scheme
예 *It was a great sales gimmick.*

ease [íːz]   *vt.* 완화시키다

🔠 lessen the intensity of or calm

🔠 alleviate, comfort, still, allay, relieve

🔠 *The news eased my conscience.*

confuse [kənfjúːz]   *vt.* 혼란시키다

🔠 cause to be perplexed or unable to think clearly.

🔠 befuddle, embarrass, confound, bewilder, perturb

🔠 *These questions confused even the experts.*

*Vocabulary/Expressions

---

translate [trænsleit] *vt.* 번역하다

图 restate (words) from one language into another language

图 render, interpret, construe, decipher, transpose

예 *She translated the French poem into English.*

---

inherent [inhíərənt] *a.* 타고난

图 existing as an essential constituent or characteristic

图 inborn, constitutional, innate, natural, inbuilt

예 *an inherent inability to tell the truth*

---

cripple [krípl] *vt.* 무능하게 하다

图 deprive of strength or efficiency

图 disable, attenuate, stultify, weaken, blunt, maim

예 *This measure crippled our efforts.*

---

reproduction [rìːprədʌkʃən] *n.* 복제

图 the act of making copies

图 replication, duplication, imitation, transcription, copy, facsimile

예 *Gutenberg's reproduction of holy texts was far more efficient.*

---

vegetation [vedʒəteiʃən] *n.* 초목

图 all the plant life in a particular region or period

图 botany, grasses, greenery, plants, flora

예 *Pleistocene vegetation*

---

appliance [əplaiəns] *n.* 기구, 전기 제품

图 a device or control that is very useful for a particular job

图 gadget, device, implement, apparatus, instrument

예 *An appliance intended to conserve water.*

---

plot [plát]   *n.* 음모

뜻 a secret scheme to do something

동 secret plan, scheme, artifice, contrivance, maneuver, stratagem, intrigue

예 *They concocted a plot to discredit the governor.*

---

captain [kǽptən]   *n.* 우두머리

뜻 the leader of a group of people

동 leader, chief, head, commander, master

예 *a captain of industry*

---

defect [di:fekt]   *n.* 결점

뜻 an imperfection in an object or machine

동 imperfection, failure, demerit, shortcoming, deficiency

예 *A defect caused the crystal to shatter.*

---

surge [sə́:rdʒ]   *vi.* 파도처럼 밀려오다, 쇄도하다, 밀어닥치다

뜻 rise and move, as in waves or billows

동 arise, swirl, pour, ripple, gush, undulate, rush

예 *The army surged forward.*

---

beverage [bevəridʒ]   *n.* 마실 것, 음료

뜻 any liquid suitable for drinking

동 drink, potable, brew, cooler

예 *May I take your beverage order?*

---

suppress [səprés]   *vt.* 억압하다

뜻 put down by force or authority

동 hold back, oppress, restrain, stamp down, inhibit, quench

예 *Suppress a nascent uprising!*

doubtful [dàutfəl]
a. 의심을 품고

图 open to doubt or suspicion

图 dubious, questionable, skeptical, uncertain, unclear

예 *He has a doubtful record indeed.*

specialty [speʃəlti]
n. 전문, 장기, 전공

图 an asset of special worth or utility

图 metier, major, career, peculiarity, strength

예 *Cooking is his specialty.*

follow [fálou]
vt. ~의 뒤를 잇다

图 travel behind, go after, come after

图 ensue, pursue, go after, succeed, attend

예 *Please follow the guide through the museum.*

employment [implɔimənt]
n. 고용

图 the occupation for which you are paid

图 work, hiring, occupying, vocation, business

예 *A lot of people are out of employment.*

burglary [bə́:rgləri]
n. 주거침입죄, 강도

图 entering a building unlawfully with intent to commit a felony or to steal valuable property

图 robbery, theft, housebreaking, sting, larceny

예 *He committed burglary.*

evaluate [ivǽljuèit]
vt. 평가하다

图 estimate the nature, quality, ability, extent, or significance of

图 appraise, test, measure, estimate, assess

예 *I will have the family jewels evaluated by a professional.*

replenish [ripléniʃ]   *vt.* 보충하다

医 fill something that had previously been emptied

동 refill, furnish, provide, refresh, fill again

예 *Replenish my glass, please.*

---

classify [klǽsəfai]   *vt.* 분류하다

医 arrange or order by classes or categories

동 categorize, sort, assort, class, separate

예 *How would you classify these pottery shards?*

---

exorbitant [igzɔ́ːrbətənt]   *a.* 엄청난

医 greatly exceeding bounds of reason or moderation

동 extravagant, excessive, inordinate, enormous, outrageous

예 *exorbitant charges*

---

resumption [rizʌ́mpʃən]   *n.* 재개

医 beginning again

동 renewal, recommencement, continuation, awakening, revival, resurrection

예 *I ordered the resumption of the meeting.*

---

probationary [proubeiʃəneri]   *a.* 시험적인, 가채용의, 견습중의

医 under terms not final or fully worked out or agreed upon

동 provisional, tentative, momentary, temporary, tested

예 *probationary employees*

---

explore [iksplɔ́ːr]   *vt.* 탐험하다

医 travel to or penetrate into

동 investigate, probe, examine, investigate, survey

예 *We are going to explore unknown territory in biology.*

ephemeral [ifémərəl] *a.* 덧없는

图 lasting a very short time

图 momentary, passing, fleeting, fugitive, temporary, transcient

예 *the ephemeral joys of childhood*

---

recruit [rikrúːt] *vt.* 모집하다

图 register formally as a participant or member

图 enlist, inscribe, enroll, enter, select

예 *The party recruited many new members.*

---

previously [príːviəsli] *adv.* 이전에

图 at an earlier time or formerly

图 earlier, before, formerly, antecedently, precedently

예 *She had previously lived in Chicago.*

---

coherent [kouhiərənt] *a.* 일관성 있는

图 marked by an orderly, logical, and aesthetically consistent relation of parts

图 consistent, ordered, logical, understandable, comprehensible

예 *a coherent argument*

---

validity [vəlídəti] *n.* 유효함; 타당성

图 the quality of having legal force or effectiveness

图 effectiveness, authority, lawfulness, efficacy, cogency, validness

예 *the term of validity*

---

redeeming [ridíːmiŋ] *a.* 보충하는

图 compensating for some fault or defect

图 redemptive, saving, compensating, offsetting

예 *The redeeming feature of the plan is its simplicity.*

order [ɔ:rdər]   *n.* 명령

圀 a command given by a superior that must be obeyed

同 command, instruction, decree, direction, mandate, charge

예 *The British ships dropped anchor and waited for orders from London.*

---

repeatedly [ripíːtidli]   *adv.* 되풀이하여

圀 more than once; again and again

同 regularly, again and again, oftentimes, time after time

예 *It must be washed repeatedly.*

---

advantage [ædvǽntidʒ]   *n.* 유리한 점

圀 the quality of having a superior or more favorable position

同 mastery, benefit, profit, prestige, supremacy

예 *The experience gave him the advantage over me.*

---

advance [ædvǽns]   *vt.* 진척시키다, 촉진하다

圀 contribute to the progress or growth of

同 proceed, promote, encourage, progress, boost

예 *I am advancing the use of computers in the classroom.*

---

conservative [kənsə́:rvətiv]   *a.* 신중한

圀 avoiding excess

同 cautious, moderate, guarded, deliberate, prudent

예 *a conservative estimate*

---

oversee [ouvərsiː]   *vt.* 감독하다

圀 watch and direct

同 inspect, monitor, control, watch, supervise

예 *Who is overseeing this project?*

verify [verəfai]　　　　　　　　　　　　　　　*vt.* 증명하다

图 confirm the truth of

동 prove, confirm, examine, corroborate, attest

예 *Please verify that the doors are closed.*

---

extra [ekstrə]　　　　　　　　　　　　　　　*a.* 여분의

图 more than needed, desired, or required

동 excess, redundant, surplus, superfluous, supernumerary

예 *Found some extra change lying on the dresser.*

---

efficiency [ifíʃənsi]　　　　　　　　　　　　*n.* 능력, 능률

图 skillfulness in avoiding wasted time and effort

동 effectiveness, proficiency, ability, skillfulness, performance

예 *She did the work with great efficiency.*

---

negotiation [nigouʃieiʃən]　　　　　　　　*n.* 협상

图 a discussion intended to produce an agreement

동 compromise, intervention, agreement, parley, mediation

예 *They disagreed but kept an open negotiation.*

---

merge [mə́:rdʒ]　　　　　　　　　　　　　　*vi.* 합병하다

图 become one

동 integrate, consolidate, amalgamate, affiliate, synthesize

예 *This department merged with another in 1990.*

---

rob [ráb]　　　　　　　　　　　　　　　　　*vt.* 강탈하다

图 take something away by force or without the consent of the owner

동 steal, deprive, embezzle, defraud, thieve

예 *The burglars robbed him of all his money.*

harassment [hərǽsmənt]   *n.* 괴롭힘

图 the act of tormenting by continued persistent attacks and criticism

图 bothering, annoyance, provoking, irking, vexing

예 *She engaged in harassment.*

legal [líːgəl]   *a.* 합법적인

图 having legal efficacy or force

图 legitimate, juridical, lawful, statutory, rightful

예 *a legal title to the property*

shift [ʃift]   *vt.* 물건을 이동시키다

图 move around

图 transfer, switch, transmit, move, displace, transpose

예 *Shift the packet from his trouser pockets to a pocket in his jacket.*

value [vǽljuː]   *n.* 가치

图 the quality (positive or negative) that renders something desirable or valuable

图 meaning, worth, usefulness, merit

예 *The Shakespearean Shylock is of dubious value in the modern world.*

faulty [fɔ́ːlti]   *a.* 결점이 있는

图 having a defect

图 defective, incorrect, deficient, erroneous, wrong, inaccurate

예 *He submitted a faulty report.*

assistant [əsístənt]   *a.* 보조의

图 of or relating to a person who is subordinate to another

图 subsidiary, auxiliary, substituting, ancillary, adjunct

예 *assistant director*

intoxicate [intʌ́ksikèit]   *vt.* 열중시키다

圐 fill with high spirits

동 excite, elate, lift up, pick up, intrigue

예 *Music can intoxicate your spirits.*

---

verification [vèrəfikéiʃən]   *n.* 증거

圐 additional proof that something that was believed (some fact or hypothesis or theory) is correct

동 proof, attestation, evidence, confirmation, substantiation

예 *Fossils provided further verification of the evolutionary theory.*

---

*Vocabulary/Expressions

immigrate [ímɡrèit]   *vi.* 이주하다
- 医 migrate to a new environment
- 동 migrate, move, emigrate, settle, come in
- 예 *Only few plants can immigrate to the island.*

rampant [rǽmpənt]   *a.* 사나운
- 医 unrestrained and violent
- 동 violent, mad, aggressive, boisterous, clamorous, outrageous
- 예 *rampant aggression*

quite [kwait]   *adv.* 아주, 완전히
- 医 to the greatest extent
- 동 absolutely, entirely, completely, really, fully
- 예 *She was quite alone.*

reimburse [ri:imbə́:rs]   *vt.* 변상하다
- 医 pay back for some expense incurred
- 동 recompense, compensate, offset, recover, indemnify
- 예 *Can the company reimburse me for my professional travel?*

attendance [əténdəns]   *n.* 참석
- 医 the act of being present (at a meeting or event etc.)
- 동 participation, presence, appearance, being there
- 예 *daily attendance*

misinterpret [mìsintə́:rprit]   *vt.* 오해하다
- 医 understand in the wrong way
- 동 misconstrue, misunderstand, distort, misapprehend, misconceive
- 예 *Don't misinterpret my comments as criticism.*

strategy [strǽtədʒi]   *n.* 전략
图 an elaborate and systematic plan of action
圖 craft, method, scenario, tactics, approach, artifice
例 *marketing strategy*

commodity [kəmádəti]   *n.* 상품
图 articles of commerce
圖 possession, goods, merchandise, thing, product
例 *commodity exchange*

whip [hwíp]   *vt.* 매질하다
图 beat severely with a whip or rod
圖 bash, tan, beat, strike, scourge
例 *The teacher often whipped the students.*

position [pəzíʃən]   *n.* 위치
图 the particular portion of space occupied by something
圖 space, place, site, location, spot
例 *He put the lamp back in its position.*

edition [idíʃən]   *n.* (출판물의) 판
图 all of the identical copies of something offered to the public at th e same time
圖 version, publication, issue, printing, variant
例 *The first edition appeared in 1920.*

variety [vəràiəti]   *n.* 종류
图 a category of things distinguished by some common characteristic or quality
圖 kind, sort, form, type, division
例 *Sculpture is a variety of art.*

impassive [impǽsiv]　　　　　　　　　　　　　*a.* 무표정한, 무감각한

图 having or revealing little emotion or sensibility not easily aroused or excited

동 expressionless, apathetic, callous, heartless, indifferent, dull

예 *His face remained impassive as the verdict was read.*

---

confront [kənfrʌnt]　　　　　　　　　　　　　*vt.* 직면하다, 맞서다

图 oppose, as in hostility or a competition

동 face, challenge, dare, affront, withstand

예 *You must confront your opponent.*

---

wield [wíːld]　　　　　　　　　　　　　　　　　*vt.* 사용하다

图 handle effectively

동 handle, manage, control, use, operate

예 *The burglar wielded an axe.*

---

embarrassing [imbǽrəsiŋ]　　　　　　　　　　*a.* 당황케하는

图 causing to feel shame or chagrin or vexation

동 shaming, perplexing, confusing, disturbing, stunning

예 *It was embarrassing to know he had heard every word.*

---

release [riliːs]　　　　　　　　　　　　　　　　*vt.* 발행하다; 방출하다

图 prepare and issue for public distribution or sale

동 publish, issue, notice, free, unbind

예 *Release a magazine or newspaper.*

---

refrain [rifrein]　　　　　　　　　　　　　　　　*vi.* 삼가다

图 resist doing something

동 inhibit, abstain, restrain withhold, forbear

예 *He refrained from hitting him back.*

unprecedented [ʌnpresədentid]
a. 전례가 없는

因 having no prior example

동 exceptional, unexampled, unparalleled, anomalous, unheard-of

예 *an unprecedented expansion in population and industry*

---

suit [suːt]
vt. 적합하다

因 be agreeable or acceptable to

동 fit, match, adjust, accommodate, befit

예 *This suits my needs.*

---

insolent [ínsələnt]
a. 건방진

因 marked by casual disrespect

동 arrogant, impudent, disrespectful, peremptory, impertinent

예 *The student was kept in for insolent behavior.*

---

completely [kəmplíːtli]
adv. 완전히

因 to the full or entire extent

동 wholly, entirely, totally, all, whole

예 *It was completely different from what we expected.*

---

allot [əlát]
vt. 할당하다

因 administer or bestow, as in small portions

동 assign, distribute, administer, dispense, share

예 *The principal allots their praise and blame impartially.*

---

board [bɔːrd]
n. 판지

因 flat piece of material designed for a special purpose

동 panel, slat, table, timber, plank

예 *He nailed boards across the windows.*

---

voluntary [váləntèri] *a.* 자발적인

뜻 of your own free will or design

동 spontaneous, natural, instinctive, casual, unconscious

예 *voluntary manslaughter*

---

impression [impréʃən] *n.* 인상, 감명

뜻 a clear and telling mental image

동 apprehension, memory, sensation, perception, thought

예 *The events left a permanent impression in his mind.*

---

flat [flǽt] *a.* 평평한

뜻 having a surface without slope, tilt in which no part is higher or lower than another

동 even, plain, level, smooth, tabular

예 *This skirts is sewn with fine flat seams.*

---

artificial [à:rtəfiʃəl] *a.* 인조의, 인공적인

뜻 contrived by art rather than nature

동 man-made, unnatural, false, unreal, factitious

예 *artificial flavoring*

---

qualification [kwàləfikeiʃən] *n.* 자격

뜻 an attribute that must be met or complied with and that fits a person for something

동 ability, aptitude, capability, reservation, fitness

예 *Her qualifications for the job are excellent.*

---

extension [iksténʃən] *n.* 확장

뜻 act of expanding in scope

동 expansion, enlargement, spread, continuation, augmentation

예 *extension of the program*

---

gusty [gʌsti]   *a.* 바람이 심한

圏 blowing in puffs or short intermittent blasts

图 puffy, windy, blowy, stormy, breezy

예 *gusty winds*

---

overlook [ouvərluk]   *vt.* 못보고 지나치다, 간과하다

圏 leave undone or leave out

图 disregard, drop, neglect, omit, miss, forget

예 *How could I overlook that typo?*

---

blend [blend]   *vt.* 섞다

圏 combine into one

图 intermix, combine, jumble, admix, stir

예 *Blend the nuts and raisins together.*

---

frustrated [frʌstreitid]   *a.* 좌절된

圏 disappointingly unsuccessful

图 discouraged, thwarted, defeated, foiled, discontented

예 *Don't give up by disappointed expectations and frustrated ambitions.*

---

collect [kəlékt]   *vt.* 모으다

圏 get or gather together

图 accumulate, pile up, amass, compile, hoard

예 *She is collecting a lot of data for her thesis.*

---

anonymous [ənánəməs]   *a.* 익명의

圏 having no known name or identity or known source

图 unnamed, innominate, concealed, nameless, incognito

예 *anonymous donors*

luggage [lʌgidʒ]　　　　　　　　　　　　　　　　　　　　*n.* 수하물

뜻 anything cumbrous and heavy to be carried, especially a traveler's trunks, baggage, etc.

동 baggage, trunk, paraphernalia, case, valise

예 *luggage handler*

condone [kəndóun]　　　　　　　　　　　　　　　　　　　*vt.* 용서하다

뜻 excuse, overlook, or make allowances for

동 forgive, overlook, excuse, pardon, remit, let pass

예 *She condoned her husband's occasional infidelities.*

prompt [prámpt]　　　　　　　　　　　　　　　　　　　　*a.* 신속한

뜻 performed with little or no delay

동 speedy, quick, rapid, expeditious, immediate

예 *a prompt reply to my letter*

accommodation [əkàmədéiʃən]　　　　　　　　　　　　　*n.* 숙박 설비

뜻 living quarters provided for public convenience

동 housing, lodging, staying, shelter, apartment, board

예 *Overnight accommodations are available.*

endorsement [indɔ́ːrsmənt]　　　　　　　　　　　　　　　*n.* 보증

뜻 formal and explicit approval

동 advocacy, authorization, support, warrant, approbation, qualification

예 *A democrat usually gets the union's endorsement.*

balanced [bǽlənst]　　　　　　　　　　　　　　　　　　　*a.* 균형잡힌

뜻 being in a state of proper equilibrium

동 regular, equalized, symmetric, proportional, well-formed

예 *a balanced assessment of intellectual and cultural history*

superior [səpiəriər]
a. 뛰어난

图 of high or superior quality or performance

图 excellent, predominant, distinguished, remarkable, surpassing

예 *Superior wisdom derives from experience.*

damage [dǽmidʒ]
vt. 손상을 가하다

图 injury or harm to person, property, or reputation

图 hurt, injure, weaken, harm, disfigure

예 *The snow damaged the roof.*

populace [pápjuləs]
n. 대중

图 people in general considered as a whole

图 public, world, population, people, rabbe

예 *He is a hero in the eyes of the populace.*

degree [digri:]
n. 정도, 등급

图 a position on a scale of intensity or amount or quality

图 rank, grade, stage, level, standard

예 *It is all a matter of degree.*

convenient [kənví:njənt]
a. 편리한

图 suited to your comfort or purpose or needs

图 comfortable, appropriate, fit, suitable, opportune

예 *a convenient excuse for not going*

vendor [vendər]
n. 행상인

图 someone who promotes or exchanges goods or services for money

图 merchant, salesperson, peddler, monger, dealer, seller

예 *a fruit vendor*

promote [prəmout]　　　　　　　　　　　　　　*vt.* 증진하다, 장려하다

图 contribute to the progress or growth of

동 encourage, boost, advance, raise, further

예 *I am promoting the use of computers in the classroom.*

---

investor [investər]　　　　　　　　　　　　　　*n.* 투자자

图 someone who commits capital in order to gain financial returns

동 shareholder, financier, capitalist, backer, stockholder

예 *institutional investor*

---

*Vocabulary/Expressions

---

scheme [skíːm]
n. 계획

- 图 an elaborate and systematic plan of action
- 图 strategy, arrangement, layout, blueprint, disposition
- 예 *Planning a scheme is very difficult.*

---

amicable [ǽmikəbl]
a. 우호적인

- 图 characterized by friendship and good will
- 图 amiable, friendly, gracious, kindly, benevolent
- 예 *amicable relations*

---

salary [sǽləri]
n. 봉급

- 图 something that remunerates
- 图 wage, pay, earnings, remuneration, stipend
- 예 *They saved a quarter of all their salaries.*

---

clarify [klǽrəfai]
vt. 뚜렷하게 하다, 명백하게 설명하다

- 图 make clear and (more) comprehensible
- 图 formulate, interprete, simplify, elucidate, define
- 예 *Clarify the mystery surrounding her death.*

---

assess [əses]
vt. 평가하다

- 图 evaluate or estimate the nature, quality, ability, extent, or significance of
- 图 measure, evaluate, appraise, estimate, value, survey
- 예 *Assess all the factors when taking a risk.*

---

complex [kəmpleks]
a. 복잡한

- 图 complicated in structure.
- 图 intricate, complicated, involved, knotty, elaborate
- 예 *This complex set of variations is based on a simple folk melody.*

---

advisor [ǽdvaizər]
n. 충고자, 조언자

㋫ an expert who gives advice

㋫ consultant, guide, mentor, helper, counselor

㋫ *An adviser helped students select their courses.*

---

enormous [inɔ́ːrməs]
a. 거대한

㋫ extraordinarily large in size or extent or amount or power or degree

㋫ great, tremendous, immense, stupendous, prodigious

㋫ *enormous expenses*

---

conductor [kəndʌ́ktər]
n. 지도자, 안내자

㋫ one who direct the couse of or manage or control

㋫ manager, director, guard, leader, guide

㋫ *Zeal is the blind conductor of the will.*

---

sporadic [spərǽdik]
a. 우발적인

㋫ recurring in scattered and irregular or unpredictable instances

㋫ intermittent, occasional, recurrent, incidental, irregular

㋫ *A city subjected to sporadic bombing raids.*

---

suspend [səspénd]
vt. 일시 중지하다

㋫ stop a process or a habit by imposing a freeze on it

㋫ discontinue, pause, cease, abandon, abort

㋫ *You must suspend the aid to the war-torn country.*

---

compact [kəmpǽkt]
a. 조밀한, 빽빽한

㋫ closely and firmly united or packed together

㋫ dense, pressed, compressed, impenetrable, crowded

㋫ *compact clusters of flowers*

sincerely [sinsíərli]   *adv.* 진정으로

图 without pretense

图 truly, seriously, honestly, really, unfeignedly

예 *We are sincerely sorry for the inconvenience.*

---

booklet [buklit]   *n.* 작은 책자

图 a small book usually having a paper cover

图 handbill, brochure, leaflet, pamphlet, folder

예 *a graduate school orientation booklet*

---

accusation [æ̀kjuzéiʃən]   *n.* 비난

图 an assertion that someone is guilty of a fault or offence

图 reproach, blame charge, censure, denunciation

예 *The newspaper published accusations that Jones was guilty of drunken driving.*

---

access [ǽkses]   *vt.* 접근하다

图 reach or gain approach to

图 reach, approach, show, visit, enter

예 *How does one access the attic in this house?*

---

general [dʒenərəl]   *a.* 일반의, 총체적인, 전반적인

图 applying to all or most members of a category or group

图 prevalent, common, normal, extensive, extensive

예 *a general rule*

---

transmit [trænsmít]   *vt.* 보내다, 전달하다

图 transfer to another

图 carry, transfer, convey, send, communicate

예 *The airwaves transmit the sound.*

stylish [stàiliʃ]   *a.* 맵시있는

图 having elegance or taste or refinement in manners or dress

圄 fashionable, chic, elegant, modish, dressy

예 *the stylish resort of Gstadd*

---

detect [ditekt]   *vt.* 발견하다

图 discover or determine the existence, presence, or fact of

圄 notice, discover, find, uncover, observe

예 *She detected high levels of lead in her drinking water.*

---

stable [steibl]   *a.* 안정된

图 resistant to change of position or condition

圄 fixed, balanced, settled, constant, steady

예 *a stable peace*

---

damp [dǽmp]   *a.* 축축한

图 slightly wet

圄 moist, wet, humid, saturated

예 *Clothes are damp with perspiration.*

---

identical [aidéntikəl]   *a.* 동일한

图 being the exact same one

圄 equal, alike, corresponding, same, tantamount

예 *This is the identical room we stayed in before.*

---

delay [dilei]   *vt.* 늦추다

图 cause to be slowed down or delayed

圄 detain, postpone, put off, defer, procrastinate, prolong

예 *Traffic was delayed by the bad weather.*

fatal [féitl]
a. 치명적인图

having extremely unfortunate or dire consequences

图 disastrous, fateful, black, calamitous, baneful

예 *a fatal defeat*

---

cooperate [kouápəreit]
vi. 협력하다

图 work together on a common enterprise of project

图 aid, collaborate, coordinate, unite, ally

예 *The soprano and the pianist did not cooperate very well.*

---

previous [prí:viəs]
a. 이전의

图 just preceding something else in time or order

图 former, anterior, precedent, foregoing, prior

예 *the previous owner*

---

cheap [tʃí:p]
a. 싼

图 relatively low in price or charging low prices

图 inexpensive, economical, low-priced, moderate, valueless

예 *cheap family restaurants*

---

spouse [spaus]
n. 배우자

图 a person's partner in marriage

图 mate, partner, married person, companion, helpmate

예 *ex-spouse*

---

hastily [héistili]
adv. 급히

图 in a hurried or hasty manner

图 hurriedly, rapidly, in haste, promptly, quickly

예 *Hastily, he scanned the headlines.*

favorite [féivərit] *a.* 마음에 드는

医 preferred above all others and treated with partiality

동 favored, preferent, beloved, pleasant, desired

예 *the favored child*

---

rebuke [ribjúːk] *vt.* 비난하다

医 censure severely or angrily

동 blame, scold, criticize, admonish, reprimand

예 *The mother rebuked the child for entering a stranger's car.*

---

attendant [əténdənt] *a.* 부수적인

医 following or accompanying as a consequence

동 consequent, accompanying, ensuant, incidental, concomitant

예 *attendant circumstances*

---

respectable [rispéktəbl] *a.* 훌륭한

医 deserving of esteem and regard

동 estimable, good, honorable, admirable, venerable

예 *All respectable companies give guarantees.*

---

gorgeous [gɔːrdʒəs] *a.* 호화스러운

医 dazzlingly beautiful

동 beautiful, magnificent, brilliant, luxurious, lavish

예 *a gorgeous Victorian gown*

---

convict [kənvikt] *vt.* 유죄를 선고하다

医 find or declare guilty

동 sentence, condemn, denounce, adjudge, doom

예 *The man was convicted of fraud and sentenced.*

gregarious [grigɛ́əriəs]   *a.* 사교적인

图 instinctively or temperamentally seeking and enjoying the company of other

图 friendly, affable, companionable, outgoing, sociable

예 *He is a gregarious person who avoids solitude.*

dispute [dispjúːt]   *vi.* 논쟁하다

图 have a disagreement over something

图 argue, contest, quarrel, clash, bicker, squable

예 *These two fellows are always disputing over something.*

subsidiary [səbsidieri]   *a.* 보조의

图 functioning in a supporting

图 supplementary, auxiliary, accessory, assistant

예 *the main library and its subsidiary branches*

reform [riːfɔ́ːrm]   *vt.* 개정하다

图 make changes for improvement in order to remove abuse and injustices

图 reclaim, amend, improve, regenerate, ameliorate, repair

예 *We reformed a political system.*

correspond [kɔːrəspánd]   *vi.* 일치하다

图 be compatible, similar or consistent

图 match, fit, accord, coincide, assimilate

예 *The two stories don't correspond in many details.*

hire [hàiər]   *vt.* 고용하다

图 engage or employ for work

图 apply, employ, use, engage, utilize

예 *They hired two new secretaries in the department.*

constituent [kənstítʃuənt]
n. 성분

图 an abstract part of something

图 component, element, factor, ingredient, part

例 *Jealousy was a component of his character.*

---

brochure [brouʃúər]
n. 팸플릿

图 a small book usually having a paper cover

图 booklet, folder, leaflet, pamphlet, flyer

例 *holiday brochure*

---

attend [əténd]
vt. 출석하다

图 be present at (meetings, church services, university), etc

图 appear, visit, be there, haunt, show

例 *She attends class regularly.*

---

license [laisəns]
n. 면허

图 a legal document giving official permission to do something

图 certificate, permission, leave, authorization

例 *driving licence*

---

territorial [tèrətɔːriəl]
a. 영토의

图 of or relating to a land

图 provincial, areal, national, sectional, regional

例 *Last week, North Korea intruded the territorial waters of South Korea.*

---

package [pǽkidʒ]
n. 꾸러미

图 a collection of things wrapped or boxed together

图 parcel, packet, bale, packing, bundle

例 *software package*

---

undergo [ʌndərgou]   *vt.* 겪다

图 pass through

图 experience, confront, encounter, face, meet, go through

예 *I underwent a strange sensation.*

transportation [trænspərtéiʃən]   *n.* 수송

图 the act of moving something from one location to another

图 carrying, portage, traffic, conveyance, passage

예 *means of transportation*

*Vocabulary/Expressions

---

resistant [rizístənt]　　　　　　　　　　　　　　*a.* 저항하는

图 able to tolerate environmental conditions or physiological stress

图 antagonistic, opposing, defiant, opposing, insusceptible

例 *The new hybrid is more resistant to drought.*

---

quote [kwóut]　　　　　　　　　　　　　　　*vt.* 인용하다

图 refer to for illustration or proof

图 cite, excerpt, reference, adduce, paraphrase

例 *He said he could quote several instances of this behavior.*

---

preside [prizaid]　　　　　　　　　　　　　　*vi.* 의장이 되다

图 act as president

图 head, administer, lead, moderate, chair

例 *He presided over companies and corporations.*

---

fiscal [fiskəl]　　　　　　　　　　　　　　*a.* 재정상의, 회계의

图 involving financial matters

图 economic, budgetary, pecuniary, commercial, pocket

例 *fiscal responsibility*

---

terribly [térəbli]　　　　　　　　　　　　　　*adv.* 무섭게

图 in a terrible manner

图 extremely, frightfully, awfully, rottenly, abominably

例 *She sings terribly.*

---

lively [làivli]　　　　　　　　　　　　　　*a.* 생기에 넘친

图 full of life and energy

图 energetic, vivacious, active, busy, spirited

例 *lively and attractive parents*

---

maintain [meintein]　　　　　　　　　　　*vt.* 유지하다

图 keep in a certain state, position, or activity

图 hold, keep up, preserve, sustain, conserve

예 *He tries to maintain his good condition.*

account [əkaunt]　　　　　　　　　　　*n.* 계산, 셈, 회계

图 a statement of recent transactions and the resulting balance

图 reckoning, computation, tally, bill

예 *They send me an account every month.*

lawsuit [lɔ:sùːt]　　　　　　　　　　　*n.* 소송

图 a comprehensive term for any proceeding in a court of law whereby an individual seeks a legal remedy

图 accusation, cause, suit, case, trial, litigation

예 *The family brought lawsuit against the landlord.*

accompany [əkʌmpəni]　　　　　　　　　　　*vt.* 동반하다

图 be present or associated with an event or entity

图 escort, attend, go with, come with

예 *Heart attacks are accompanied by distruction of heart tissue.*

deserve [dizə́:rv]　　　　　　　　　　　*vt.* ~할(받을) 만하다

图 be worthy or deserving

图 merit, earn, rate, be entitled to

예 *You deserve a promotion after all the hard work you have done.*

contract [kántrækt]　　　　　　　　　　　*n.* 계약

图 a binding agreement between two or more persons that is enforceable by law

图 treaty, pact, convention, engagement

예 *breach of contract*

investment [invéstmənt]   *n.* 투자

图 laying out money or capital in an enterprise with the expectation of profit

图 finance, funding, backing, expenditure, asset, venture

예 *overseas investments*

feasible [fíːzəbl]   *a.* 실행할 수 있는

图 capable of being done with means at hand and circumstances as they are

图 workable, likely, executable, practicable, possible, viable

예 *a feasible project*

manual [mǽnjuəl]   *n.* 소책자, 취급 설명서, 편람, 안내서

图 a small handbook

图 guidebook, compendium, enchiridion, instruction

예 *The audiences are reading the manual.*

dismantle [dismǽntl]   *vt.* 분해하다

图 take apart into its constituent pieces

图 piece, decompose, strike, disassemble, strip

예 *The scenery was dismantled.*

adept [ədépt]   *a.* 숙달한

图 having or showing knowledge and skill and aptitude

图 proficient, expert, good, practiced, skillful

예 *an adept juggler*

concerned [kənsə́ːrnd]   *a.* 걱정스러운

图 feeling or showing worry or solicitude

图 worried, uneasy, anxious, solicitous, attentive

예 *concerned parents of youthful offenders*

area [ɛ́əriə]　　　　　　　　　　　　　　　　　　　　*n.* 지역

뜻 a particular geographical region of indefinite boundary

동 region, district, field, zone, territory

예 *It was a mountainous area.*

---

reduction [ridʌ́kʃən]　　　　　　　　　　　　　　　*n.* 축소

뜻 the act of decreasing or reducing something

동 diminution, decline, subdual, abatement, contraction, curtailment

예 *weight reduction*

---

squint [skwínt]　　　　　　　　　　　　　　　*vi.* 곁눈질하다

뜻 cross one's eyes as if in strabismus

동 peek, look askance, squinch, look, peep

예 *The children squinted so as to scare each other.*

---

security [sikjúərəti]　　　　　　　　　　　　　　*n.* 안전

뜻 the state of being free from danger or injury

동 assurance, safeguard, protection, pledge, safety

예 *We support the armed services in the name of national security.*

---

remarkable [rimá:rkəbl]　　　　　　　　　　　　*a.* 주목할 만한

뜻 worthy of notice

동 noteworthy, extraordinary, unusual, outstanding, peculiar

예 *a remarkable achievement*

---

deterrent [ditə́:rənt]　　　　　　　　　　　　　　*n.* 방해물

뜻 something immaterial that interferes with or delays action or progress

동 hindrance, impediment, obstacle, handicap, barrier

예 *an effective deterrent*

---

opposition [àpəzíʃən] *n.* 반대

图 the action of resisting something that you disapprove or disagree with

图 resistance, obstruction, antagonism, aversion, contest

예 *Despite opposition from the newspapers, he went ahead.*

---

attention [ətenʃən] *n.* 주의, 주목

图 the process whereby a person concentrates on some features of the environment to the (relative) exclusion of others

图 notice, concentration, concern, awareness, consciousness

예 *He gave attention to her.*

---

cumulative [kjuːmjulətiv] *a.* 누적하는

图 increasing by successive addition

图 collective, accumulative, increasing, multiplying

예 *the eventual cumulative effect of these substances*

---

stuffy [stʌfi] *a.* 지루한

图 excessively conventional and unimaginative and hence dull

图 dull, irksome, routine, stodgy, uninteresting

예 *a stuffy dinner party*

---

interior [intíəriər] *a.* 내부의

图 located inward

图 inner, inside, central, domestic, internal

예 *an interior sense of rightousness*

---

entertain [èntərtéin] *vt.* 즐겁게 하다

图 provide entertainment for

图 divert, amuse, gratify, please, cheer

예 *He entertained guests.*

exploit [ikspl3it]
vt. 이용하다

图 use or manipulate to one's advantage

图 engage, use, practice, utilize, operate

예 *She knows how to exploit the system.*

---

ensure [inʃúər]
vt. 확실하게하다

图 be careful or certain to do something

图 guarantee, assure, indemnify, confirm, secure

예 *He ensured that the valves were closed.*

---

purchase [pə́:rtʃəs]
vt. 사다

图 acquire by means of a financial transaction

图 get, buy, obtain, take, procure

예 *The family purchased a new car.*

---

penetrate [penətreit]
vt. 꿰뚫다

图 pass into or through, often by overcoming resistance

图 pierce, infiltrate, go through, permeate, force

예 *The bullet penetrated her chest.*

---

proposal [prəpóuzəl]
n. 제안

图 that which is propounded for consideration or acceptance

图 proposition, suggestion, plan, recommendation

예 *They listened to her proposal.*

---

literate [lítərət]
a. 글을 읽고 쓸 줄 아는

图 able to read and write

图 cultivated, learned, educated, lettered, cultured

예 *literate person*

---

witness [wítnis]　　　　　　　　　　　　　　　　　　*vt.* 목격하다

医 give testimony to

동 testify, attest, find, vouch, certify

예 *She witnessed the accident and had to testify in court.*

---

custom [kʌstəm]　　　　　　　　　　　　　　　　　　*n.* 습관

医 accepted or habitual practice

동 practice, habit, routine, addiction, consuetude, usage, praxis

예 *Custom is second nature.*

---

enclose [inklouz]　　　　　　　　　　　　　　　　　*vt.* 에워싸다

医 enclose or enfold completely with or as if with a covering

동 surround, encircle, enfold, wrap

예 *Fog enclosed the house.*

---

supervise [sú:pərvàiz]　　　　　　　　　　　　　　*vt.* 감독하다

医 watch and direct

동 monitor, control, inspect, watch, oversee

예 *Who is supervising this project?*

---

venture [ventʃər]　　　　　　　　　　　　　　　　　*n.* 모험

医 the risking of something upon an e vent which can not be foreseen with certainty

동 adventure, hazard, risk, gamble, attempt

예 *Venture into the unknown is so funny.*

---

benign [binàin]　　　　　　　　　　　　　　　　　　*a.* 친절한

医 kindness of disposition or manner

동 kindly, amiable, beneficent, merciful, gracious

예 *benign intentions*

---

habitation [hǽbitei∫ən]   *n.* 거주지

図 housing that someone is living in

동 dwelling, home, domicile, residency, abode

예 *He built a modest habitation near the pond.*

---

split [splít]   *vt.* 쪼개다

図 separate into parts or portions

동 divide, separate, cleave, disjoin, rip

예 *Split the cake into three equal parts.*

---

swallow [swάlou]   *vt.* 삼키다, 들이키다

図 pass through the esophagus as part of eating or drinking

동 engulf, devour, gulp, ingest, drink

예 *You can swallow the raw fish--it won't kill you!*

---

return [ritə́:rn]   *vi.* 되돌아가다

図 go or come back to place, condition, or activity where one has been before

동 turn back, rebound, back up, revert, retrace, revisit

예 *Return to your native land.*

---

isolate [àisəlèit]   *vt.* 고립시키다

図 place or set apart

동 segregate, detach. insulate, seclude, withdraw

예 *They isolated the political prisoners from the other inmates.*

---

hinder [híndər]   *vt.* 방해하다

図 prevent the progress or accomplishment of

동 obstruct, blockade, embarrass, prevent

예 *His brother hindered him at every turn.*

---

remit [rimit]　　　　　　　　　　　　　　　　　　　　　*vt.* 보내다, 송금하다

圐 send (money) in payment

통 transfer, mail, post, transmit, dispatch

예 *I remited $25 to my family in Korea.*

suggest [səgdʒest]　　　　　　　　　　　　　　　　　　*vt.* 제안하다

圐 make a proposal, declare a plan for something

통 propose, submit, advise, pose, put, recommend

예 *The senator suggested to abolish the sales tax.*

*Vocabulary/Expressions

Day 27

frankly [frǽŋkli]

adv. 솔직히

- 图 it is sincerely the case that
- 图 truly, honestly, candidly, openly, veraciously
- 例 *Frankly, I don't believe it.*

predecessor [prédəsèsər]

n. 전임자

- 图 something that precedes and indicates the approach of something or someone
- 图 prior, antecedent, forerunner, herald, precursor
- 例 *immediate predecessor*

advertisement [æ̀dvərtàizmənt]

n. 광고

- 图 a public promotion of some product or service
- 图 advertizing, commercial, broadcast, promotion
- 例 *self-advertisement*

article [ɑ́:rtikl]

n. 물품

- 图 nonfictional prose forming an independent part of a publication
- 图 object, commodity, section, thing, item
- 例 *articles of stationery*

allegation [æ̀ligeiʃən]

n. 주장, 변증

- 图 a formal accusation against somebody
- 图 affirmation, assertion, contention, statement, claim
- 例 *an allegation of malpractice*

deficit [défəsit] *n.* 부족

图 the property of being an amount by which something is less than expected or required

图 deficiency, insufficiency, shortage, paucity, scantiness

예 *nutritional deficit*

---

adverse [ædvə́ːrs] *a.* 반대의

图 in an opposing direction

图 opposite, contrary, negative, reverse, repugnant

예 *adverse currents*

---

apology [əpálədʒi] *n.* 사과

图 an expression of regret at having caused trouble for someone

图 excuse, pardon, atonement, vindication

예 *He wrote a letter of apology to the hostess.*

---

dwell [dwél] *vi.* 거주하다

图 inhabit or live in

图 live, inhabit, reside, populate, stay

예 *People dwelled in Africa millions of years ago.*

---

oscillate [ásəlèit] *vi.* 진동하다

图 move or swing from side to side regularly

图 vibrate, sway, vacillate, fluctuate, wave

예 *The needle on the meter was oscillating.*

---

seek [síːk] *vt.* 추구하다

图 make an effort or attempt

图 endeavor, attempt, strive, aim, try

예 *She always seeks to do good in the world.*

pour [pɔ:r] *vi.* 흐르듯이 이동하다

图 move in large numbers

동 stream, swarm, teem, pullulate, overflow

예 *People were pouring out of the theater.*

pressure [préʃər] *n.* 압박

图 a force that compels

동 compulsion, push, oppression, tension, strain

예 *The public brought pressure to bear on the government.*

muggy [mʌgi] *a.* 무더운

图 hot or warm and humid

동 steamy, humid, moist, sultry, sticky, stuffy

예 *muggy weather*

shrink [ʃríŋk] *vi.* 움츠러지다

图 draw back, as with fear or pain

동 flinch, squinch, cringe, wince, quail

예 *She shrinked when they showed the slaughtering of the calf.*

lucrative [lu:krətiv] *a.* 유리한, 돈이 벌리는

图 producing a sizeable profit

동 profitable, moneymaking, beneficial, productive, remunerative

예 *a lucrative business*

insidious [insídiəs] *a.* 교활한

图 beguiling but harmful

동 sneaky, tricky, deceptive, crafty, treacherous

예 *insidious pleasures*

friction [frikʃən]
n. (의견)충돌

- 医 a state of conflict between persons
- 동 disagreement, quarrel, dissention, wrangling, hostility
- 예 *friction with another country*

compliment [kámpləmənt]
vt. 칭찬하다

- 医 say something to someone that expresses praise
- 동 commend, felicitate, congratulate, praise
- 예 *He complimented her on her last physics paper.*

candidate [kǽndidèit]
n. 후보자, 지원자

- 医 someone who is considered for something (for an office or prize or honor etc.)
- 동 applicant, nominee, aspirant, postulant, seeker
- 예 *a presidential candidate*

regardless [rigáːrdlis]
a. 부주의한, 관심없는

- 医 without due thought or consideration
- 동 indifferent, careless, unconcerned, inattentive, heedless
- 예 *He is regardless of the incident.*

session [seʃən]
n. 개회, 회의

- 医 a meeting for execution of a group's functions
- 동 assembly, conference, gathering, concourse, sitting
- 예 *It was the opening session of the legislature.*

depreciate [dipríːʃièit]
vt. 가치를 저하시키다

- 医 lower the value of something
- 동 undervalue, devaluate, abate, depress, worsen
- 예 *The Fed depreciated the dollar once again.*

submission [səbmíʃən]   *n.* 복종

图 the condition of having submitted to control by someone or something else

图 obedience, surrender, yielding, resignation, acquiescence

예 *His submission to the will of God is too strong.*

allotment [əlátmənt]   *n.* 할당, 분배

图 the act of distributing by apportioning

图 apportioning, allocation, distribution, share, parceling

예 *the allotment of seats*

interest [íntərəst]   *n.* 관심, 흥미

图 a sense of concern with and curiosity about someone or something

图 concern, notice, curiosity, preoccupation, attention

예 *an interest in music*

moist [mɔist]   *a.* 축축한

图 slightly wet

图 damp, humid, wet, soggy, dank

예 *Clothes are moist with perspiration.*

suspect [səspekt]   *vt.* 짐작하다

图 imagine to be the case or true or probable

图 doubt, presume, guess, reckon, distrust, speculate

예 *I suspect he is a fugitive.*

endorse [indɔ:rs]   *vt.* 어음·증권 등에 배서하다

图 sign as evidence of legal transfer

图 indorse, countersign, autograph

예 *He endorsed cheques.*

retaliate [ritǽlièit]　　　　　　　　　　　　　　*vt.* 보복하다

医 take revenge for a perceived wrong

통 revenge, avenge, vindicate, chastise, punish

예 *He wants to retaliate the murderer of his brother.*

---

revenue [revənju:]　　　　　　　　　　　　　　*n.* 세입

医 the entire amount of income before any deductions are made

통 earnings, profit, income, proceeds, emolument

예 *He defrauded the revenue.*

---

amazing [əméiziŋ]　　　　　　　　　　　　　　*a.* 놀랄만한

医 inspiring awe or admiration or wonder

통 awesome, astonishing, fascinating, awful, wonderful

예 *New York is an amazing city.*

---

lengthen [léŋkθən]　　　　　　　　　　　　　　*vt.* 길게하다

医 make longer

통 extend, stretch, expand, amplify, prolong

예 *Lengthen this skirt, please.*

---

drastic [drǽstik]　　　　　　　　　　　　　　*a.* 격렬한

医 forceful and extreme and rigorous

통 forceful, severe, extreme, radical, immoderate

예 *drastic measures*

---

invest [invést]　　　　　　　　　　　　　　*vt.* 투자하다

医 provide with power and authority

통 entrust, devote, plunge, endow, buy stock

예 *They invested the council with special rights.*

243

sabotage [sǽbətà:ʒ]　　　　　　　　　　*vt.* 고의로 파괴하다

图 destroy property or hinder normal operations

图 incapacitate, damage, undermine, counteract, wreck

예 *The Resistance sabotaged railroad operations during the war.*

---

subtract [səbtrǽkt]　　　　　　　　　　*vt.* ~에서 빼다

图 take off or away

图 withdraw, deduct, withhold, abstract, detract

예 *Subtract this amount from my paycheck.*

---

establish [istǽbliʃ]　　　　　　　　　　*vt.* 설립하다

图 set up or found

图 organize, institute, settle, constitute, base

예 *She establishes a literacy program.*

---

defendant [diféndənt]　　　　　　　　　　*n.* 피고인

图 a person or institution against whom an action is brought in a court of law

图 accused, culprit, suspect, respondent, indictee

예 *arraigned defendant*

---

imperative [impérətiv]　　　　　　　　　　*a.* 피할 수 없는

图 requiring attention or action

图 necessary, urgent, vital, crucial, important

예 *I hate your imperative tone of voice.*

---

vigilant [vídʒələnt]　　　　　　　　　　*a.* 경계하고 있는

图 carefully observant or attentive

图 careful, watchful, observant, acute, wakeful

예 *the vigilant eye of the town watch*

---

branch [brǽntʃ]   *n.* 부문

图 a division of some larger or more complex organization

图 category, subdivision, department, bureau, arm

예 the *Germanic branch of Indo-European languages*

---

conclude [kənklu:d]   *vt.* 결론짓다

图 draw or come to a conclusion

图 end, finish, terminate, consummate, desist

예 *We concluded that it was cheaper to rent than to buy a house.*

---

clash [klǽʃ]   *vi.* 충돌하다

图 crash together with violent impact

图 collide, bang, crash, smash, grind, rattle

예 *Two meteors clashed.*

---

integrate [intəgreit]   *vt.* 통합하다

图 make into a whole or make part of a whole

图 combine, amalgamate, merge, unite, embody

예 *She integrated his suggestions into her proposal.*

---

influx [ínflʌks]   *n.* 유입

图 the process of flowing in

图 incoming, afflux, flow, inrush, inflow

예 *influx of capital*

---

incoherent [ìnkouhíərənt]   *a.* 모순된

图 without logical or meaningful connection

图 inconsistent, unintelligible, discordant, incomprehensible, conflicting

예 *a turgid incoherent presentation*

245

product [prádʌkt]

n. 생산품

图 commodities offered for sale

图 merchandise, commodity, manufacture, output, ware

예 *Good business depends on having good product.*

---

fancy [fænsi]

vt. 공상하다

图 see in one's mind

图 conceive, like, suppose, imagine, think

예 *I can fancy what will happen.*

---

ungrateful [ʌngréitfəl]

a. 배은망덕의

图 not feeling or showing gratitude

图 thankless, unthankful, ingrate, oblivious, selfish

예 *ungrateful heirs*

*Vocabulary/Expressions Day 28

---

assessment [əsésmənt] *n.* 평가

图 the act of judging or evaluating a person or situation or event

图 judgement, evaluation, appraisal, estimate

例 *They criticized my assessment of the contestants.*

---

distinguish [distíŋgwiʃ] *vt.* 구별하다

图 mark as different

图 discriminate, differentiate, separate, characterize, discern

例 *We can distinguish several kinds of maple.*

---

denote [dinout] *vt.* 나타내다

图 be a sign or indication of

图 mark, indicate, designate, show, mean

例 *Her smile denoted that she agreed.*

---

covetous [kʌvitəs] *a.* 탐욕스러운

图 showing extreme cupidity

图 envious, greedy, jealous, avaricious, prehensile

例 *He was never covetous before he met her.*

---

acquit [əkwit] *vt.* 무죄로 하다

图 pronounce not guilty of criminal charges

图 release, discharge, exculpate, assoil, clear, exonerate

例 *The suspect was acquited of the murder charges.*

---

emphasize [émfəsàiz] *vt.* 강조하다

图 stress, single out as important

图 underline, accentuate, stress, underscore, punctuate

例 *Dr. Jones emphasizes exercise in addition to a change in diet.*

---

posterity [pɑstérəti]   *n.* 후세

- 图 all future generations
- 图 descendants, offspring, successors, unborn, progeniture
- 例 *This land has to be preserved for our posterity.*

---

expand [ikspǽnd]   *vi.* 팽창하다

- 图 extend in one or more directions
- 图 magnify, augment, amplify, extend, spread
- 例 *The dough expands.*

---

accuse [əkjuːz]   *vt.* 고발하다

- 图 level a chare against
- 图 denounce, impeach, censure, inculpate, incriminate
- 例 *The neighbors accused the man of spousal abuse.*

---

opponent [əpóunənt]   *n.* 반대자

- 图 someone who takes a contrary position
- 图 antagonist, competitor, rival, enemy, foe
- 例 *He designated his opponents.*

---

habitat [hǽbitæt]   *n.* 거주지

- 图 the type of environment in which an organism or group normally lives or occurs
- 图 domicile, territory, abode, house, occupation
- 例 *He feels safe only in his habitat.*

---

plentiful [pléntifəl]   *a.* 풍부한

- 图 affording an abundant supply
- 图 abundant, productive, ample, bountiful, sufficient, rich
- 例 *plentiful provisions*

---

mobile [móubəl]   *a.* 이동할 수 있는

图 moving or capable of moving readily

图 movable, portable, moving, travelling

예 *a mobile missile system*

---

leap [líːp]   *vi.* 껑충뛰다

图 move forward by leaps and bounds

图 bounce, hop, spring, jump, vault

예 *The child leapt across the puddle.*

---

panic [pǽnik]   *n.* 공포, 공황

图 sudden mass fear and anxiety over anticipated events

图 scare, alarm, terror, affright, fright

예 *panic in the stock market*

---

insulate [ínsəlèit]   *vt.* 격리하다

图 place or set apart

图 isolate, sever, detach, quarantine, seclude

예 *They insulated the political prisoners from the other inmates.*

---

defection [difékʃən]   *n.* (조국 등을) 저버림

图 withdrawing support or help despite allegiance or responsibility

图 desertion, abandonment, negligence, default, carelessness

예 *His defection of his wife and children left them penniless.*

---

pessimistic [pesəmistik]   *a.* 비관적인

图 expecting the worst possible outcome

图 cynical, hopeless, distrustful, depressed, misanthropic

예 *She takes a pessimistic view of them.*

moral [mɔ́ːrəl]   *a.* 도덕의

图 concerned with principles of right and wrong or conforming to standards of behavior and character based on those principles

동 ethic, righteous, innocent, virtuous

예 *moral sense*

---

spread [spréd]   *vt.* 퍼뜨리다

图 cause to become widely known

동 propagate, diffuse, circulate, distribute, disseminate

예 *I spread the information.*

---

organize [ɔ́ːrgənaiz]   *vt.* 조직하다

图 create as an entity

동 systematize, arrange, construct, formulate

예 *They organized a company.*

---

involve [inválv]   *vt.* 포함하다

图 contain as a part

동 include, contain, comprise, incorporate, imply

예 *Dinner at Joe's always involves at least six courses.*

---

flaw [flɔː]   *n.* 흠, 결점

图 an imperfection in an object or machine

동 fault, crack, defect, stain, imperfection

예 *A flaw caused the crystal to shatter.*

---

legacy [légəsi]   *n.* 유산

图 a gift of personal property by will

동 inheritance, patrimony, heritage, estate, bequest

예 *legacy duty*

---

velocity [vəlásəti]   *n.* 속도

图 distance travelled per unit time

동 pace, speed, quickness, rate, tempo

예 *accelerated velocity*

---

hazy [héizi]   *a.* 애매한

图 indistinct or hazy in outline

동 bleary, foggy, blurry, fuzzy, muzzy

예 *The trees were just hazy shapes.*

---

plummet [plʌmit]   *vi.* 폭락하다

图 drop sharply

동 decline, plunge, fall, collapse, drop

예 *The stock market plummeted.*

---

retrieve [ritri:v]   *vt.* 되찾다

图 get or find back

동 regain, recover, find, recapture, repossess

예 *She retrieved her voice and replied quickly.*

---

conceive [kənsí:v]   *vi.* 상상하다

图 have the idea for

동 imagine, believe, fancy, consider, think

예 *He conceived of a robot that would help paralyzed patients.*

---

corridor [kɔ:ridər]   *n.* 복도, 회랑

图 an enclosed passageway

동 passage, hallway, couloir, aisle, entranceway

예 *air corridor*

Day 28

provision [prəvíʒən]   *n.* 조항, 규정
圆 a stipulated condition
동 term, condition, proviso, stipulation, clause
예 *He accepted subject to one provision.*

frenzy [frénzi]   *n.* 격분
圆 state of violent mental agitation
동 rage, agitation, madness, outburst, craze, fury
예 *He worked himself into a frenzy.*

outgoing [àutgòuiŋ]   *a.* 외향적인
圆 at ease in talking to others
동 extroverted, forthcoming, approachable, sociable, friendly
예 *My ideal style is an outgoing girl.*

sort [sɔːrt]   *n.* 종류
圆 a category of things distinguished by some common characteristic or quality
동 kind, category, species, class, type
예 *Sculpture is a sort of art.*

amuse [əmjúːz]   *vt.* 재미있게 하다
圆 make somebody laugh
동 recreate, entertain, divert, regale, tickle
예 *The clown amused the children.*

secret [síːkrit]   *a.* 비밀의
圆 conducted with or marked by hidden aims or methods
동 hidden, clandestine, privy, furtive, undercover
예 *secret missions*

respire [rispàiər]   *vi.* 호흡하다

医 draw air into, and expel out of, the lungs

동 breathe, take a breath, inhale, oxidate, suspire

예 *The patient is respiring.*

---

display [displei]   *vt.* 전시하다, 진열하다, 장식하다

医 show, make visible or apparent

동 expose, exhibit, show, demonstrate, illustrate

예 *National leaders will have to display the highest skills of statesmanship.*

---

correspondence [kɔ:rəspándəns]   *n.* 일치, 조화

医 compatibility of observations

동 coherence, accord, coincidence, agreement, concurrence

예 *The results of two tests were in correspondence.*

---

sophisticated [səfistəkeitid]   *a.* 정교한

医 ahead in development

동 intricate, advanced, elaborate, complicated, refined

예 *sophisticated technology*

---

congregation [kàŋgrigéiʃən]   *n.* 모임

医 an assemblage of people or animals or things collected together

동 aggregation, muster, gathering, collection, meeting

예 *A great congregation of birds flew over.*

---

inevitable [inevətəbl]   *a.* 피할 수 없는

医 incapable of being avoided or prevented

동 necessary, ineluctable, unavoidable, fatal, inescapable

예 *the inevitable result*

scorch [skɔ:rtʃ]　　　　　　　　　　　　　　　　　*vt.* 태우다

- 图 burn slightly and superficially so as to affect color
- 图 burn, roast, blacken, sear, broil
- 몡 *The fire scorched the ceiling above the mantelpiece.*

besides [bisaidz]　　　　　　　　　　　　　　　　　*adv.* 게다가

- 图 making an additional point
- 图 moreover, furthermore, also, further, in addition
- 몡 *I don't want to go to a restaurant, besides we can't afford it.*

riot [ràiət]　　　　　　　　　　　　　　　　　*vi.* 폭동을 일으키다

- 图 disturb the public peace by engaging in a riot
- 图 protest, fight, revolt, arise, rampage
- 몡 *Students were rioting everywhere in 1968.*

inclement [inkləmənt]　　　　　　　　　　　*a.* 날씨가 험한, 혹독한, 추운

- 图 (of weather or climate) severe
- 图 severe, harsh, cold, rigorous, tempestuous
- 몡 *inclement weather*

compile [kəmpail]　　　　　　　　　　　　　　　*vt.* 수집하다

- 图 get or gather together
- 图 collect, accumulate, congregate, amass, muster
- 몡 *She compiled a small fortune.*

correspondent [kɔ:rəspándənt]　　　　　　　*n.* 특파원, 통신원

- 图 a journalist employed to provide news stories for newspapers or broadcast media
- 图 reporter, newspaperman, pressman, newswriter, stringer
- 몡 *war correspondent*

nearby [níərbài]   *a.* 가까운

图 close at hand

图 adjacent, proximate, adjoining, neighboring, close

예 *the nearby towns*

---

abolish [əbáliʃ]   *vt.* 폐지하다

图 do away with

图 nullify, abrogate, annihilate, eradicate, invalidate, put an end to

예 *Slavery was abolished in the mid-19th century in America and in Russia.*

---

*Vocabulary/Expressions

---

extravagant [ikstrǽvəgənt]　　　　　　　　*a.* 낭비하는

图 recklessly wasteful

图 indulgent, wasteful, excessive, prodigal, spendthrift, profligate

예 *He is extravagant in their expenditures.*

---

ahead [əhed]　　　　　　　　*prep.* 앞쪽에

图 at or in the front

图 precedent, advanced, fore, previous, onward

예 *The road ahead is foggy.*

---

hatred [héitrid]　　　　　　　　*n.* 증오

图 the emotion of intense dislike

图 hate, hostility, aversion, antipathy, distaste, malice

예 *race hatred*

---

dreadful [drédfəl]　　　　　　　　*a.* 무서운

图 causing fear or dread or terror

图 fearful, awful, dire, horrific, frightening

예 *a dreadful storm*

---

guess [gés]　　　　　　　　*vt.* 추측하다

图 expect, believe, or suppose

图 think, opine, suppose, imagine, reckon, calculate

예 *I guess she is angry at me for standing her up.*

---

gratitude [grǽtətjùːd]　　　　　　　　*n.* 감사

图 a feeling of thankfulness and appreciation

图 thankfulness, acknowledgment, appreciation, praise

예 *He was overwhelmed with gratitude for their help.*

---

support [səpɔ́ːrt]   *vt.* 지지하다

영 support materially or financially

동 sustain, maintain, uphold, prop, keep

예 *The scholarship supported me when I was in college.*

---

define [difàin]   *vt.* 뜻을 명확히 하다

영 decide upon or fix definitely

동 fix, determine, set, limit, specify

예 *We defined the parameters.*

---

fabulous [fǽbjuləs]   *a.* 전설상의

영 based on or told of in traditional stories

동 fabled, legendary, fantastic, mythical, fantastical

예 *I want to see the fabulous unicorn.*

---

soak [sóuk]   *vi.* 적시다

영 submerge in a liquid

동 drench, saturate, absorb, sop, wet

예 *I soaked in the hot tub for an hour.*

---

retard [ritáːrd]   *vt.* 속력을 늦추다

영 cause to move more slowly or operate at a slower rate

동 delay, slow down, defer, detain, postpone, impede

예 *This drug will retard your heart rate.*

---

superfluous [suːpə́ːrfluəs]   *a.* 여분의

영 more than is needed, desired, or required

동 excess, redundant, extra, surplus, supererogatory

예 *She was trying to lose superfluous weight.*

fidgety [fídʒiti] *a.* 안절부절 못하는
图 nervous and unable to relax
图 restless, itchy, nervous, impatient, antsy, fretful
예 *a fidgety child*

dictate [dikteit] *vt.* 구술하다
图 say out loud for the purpose of recording
图 state, pronounce, say, instruct
예 *He dictated a report to his secretary.*

organization [ɔ:rgənizeiʃən] *n.* 조직, 구성
图 a group of people who work together
图 system, assembly, institution, unity, constitution
예 *nongovernmental organization*

diploma [diploumə] *n.* 졸업증서
图 a document certifying the successful completion of a course of study
图 degree, confirmation, certificate, recognition, charter, credentials
예 *a high-school diploma*

deem [dí:m] *vt.* 생각하다
图 keep in mind or convey as a conviction or view
图 consider, reckon, hold, view as, take for
예 *I deem him personally responsible.*

select [silékt] *vt.* 고르다
图 pick out, select, or choose from a number of alternatives
图 choose, pick, opt, take, cull, sort out
예 *She selected a pair of shoes from among the dozen which the salesman had shown to her.*

deposit [dipάzit] *vt.* 두다

医 put something somewhere firmly

동 locate, place, lay, lodge, settle

예 *Deposit the suitcase on the bench.*

---

amenity [əmenəti] *n.* 기분에 맞음

医 pleasantness resulting from agreeable conditions

동 agreeableness, delightfulness, mildness, enjoyableness, pleasantness

예 *He discovered the amenities of reading at an early age.*

---

plague [pléig] *vt.* 괴롭히다

医 annoy continually or chronically

동 harass, annoy, bother, chevy, molest, provoke

예 *He is known to plague his staff when he is overworked.*

---

disturb [distə́:rb] *vt.* 방해하다, 어지럽히다

医 destroy the peace or tranquility of

동 interrupt, bother, interfere, commove, depress

예 *Don't disturb me when I'm reading!*

---

audit [ɔ́:dit] *vt.* (회계를) 감사하다

医 examine carefully for accuracy with the intent of verification

동 scrutinize, inspect, invertigate, go through, verify

예 *I audit accounts and tax returns.*

---

defeat [difí:t] *vt.* 쳐부수다, 패배시키다

医 win a victory over

동 overcome, beat, conquer, overpower, vanquish

예 *Defeat your enemies, my son!*

confidential [kànfədénʃəl]
a. 기밀의

图 (of information) given in confidence or in secret

图 classified, secret, intimate, arcane, clandestine

예 *This arrangement must be kept confidential.*

broadcast [brɔ:dkǽst]
vt. (소문을) 퍼뜨리다

图 cause to become widely known

图 diffuse, spread, propagate, disseminate, transmit

예 *He broadcasts information to them.*

liquidate [likwideit]
vt. 청산하다

图 eliminate by paying off

图 recompense, clear, reimburse, pay, repay

예 *She liquidated the past.*

administer [ædministər]
vt. 관리하다

图 supervise or be in charge of

图 direct, govern, manage, conduct, supervise, oversee

예 *She administers the funds.*

assignment [əsainmənt]
n. 할당

图 the act of distributing something to designated places or persons

图 allocation, assignation, quota, allotment, rationing

예 *The first task is the assignment of an address to each datum.*

hearty [háːrti]
a. 마음에서 우러난

图 showing warm and heartfelt friendliness

图 cordial, warmhearted, heartfelt, earnest, sincere

예 *a hearty welcome*

garbage [gá:rbidʒ]   *n.* 음식찌꺼기, 쓰레기

图 food that is discarded as from a kitchen

图 trash, litter, junk, rubbish, offal

예 *garbage can*

---

wondrous [wʌndrəs]   *a.* 놀랄만한

图 extraordinarily good or great

图 tremendous, marvelous, wonderful, grand, howling

예 *a wondrous collection of rare books*

---

awareness [əwéərnis]   *n.* 자각, 인식

图 having knowledge of

图 consciousness, knowingness, realization, cognisance

예 *He had no awareness of his mistakes.*

---

vehicle [ví:ikl]   *n.* 탈것

图 a conveyance that transports people or objects

图 transport, car, wheels, conveyance, carriage

예 *This vehicle is so good to me. I'll take this!*

---

reconcile [rekənsail]   *vt.* 조정하다, 중재하다

图 make one thing compatible with another

图 accommodate, adjust, attune, conciliate, regulate

예 *The scientists had to reconcile the new results with the existing theories.*

---

institute [instətju:t]   *vt.* 세우다, 설립하다

图 set up or lay the groundwork for

图 found, establish, plant, constitute, set up

예 *He instituted a new department.*

modify [mádəfai]
vt. 변경하다, 수정하다

圏 cause to change

圄 alter, transform, adapt, revise, correct

엔 *The discussion has modified my thinking about the issue.*

hurry [hə́:ri]
vi. 서두르다

圏 act or move at high speed

圄 rush, expedite, hasten, accelerate, hustle, burst

엔 *We have to hurry!*

sanction [sǽŋkʃən]
n. 허용

圏 formal and explicit approval

圄 approval, permission, endorsement, authorization, ratification

엔 *A Democrat usually gets the union's snaction.*

strike [straik]
vt. 치다, 때리다

圏 hit against

圄 smash, bang, clash, pound, punch, hammer

엔 *He struck the table with his elbow.*

relatively [rélətivli]
adv. 상대적으로

圏 by comparison to something else

圄 comparatively, rather, approximately, proportionately, somewhat

엔 *The situation is relatively calm now.*

repay [ri:péi]
vt. 갚다

圏 pay back

圄 compensate, give back, pay back, refund, return

엔 *Please repay me my money.*

extinct [ikstiŋkt]   *a.* 사라진; 멸종한

- 图 no longer in existence
- 图 dead, obsolete, defunct, nonextant, vanished, archaic
- 예 *extinct laws and customs*

widespread [waidspred]   *a.* 널리 보급된

- 图 widely circulated or diffused
- 图 extensive, universal, prevalent, comprehensive, broad
- 예 *a widespread doctrine*

reduce [ridjúːs]   *vt.* 줄이다

- 图 cut down on
- 图 diminish, lessen, abate, decrease, lower
- 예 *Reduce your daily fat intake.*

catastrophe [kətǽstrəfi]   *n.* 대참사

- 图 an event resulting in great loss and misfortune
- 图 disaster, calamity, tragedy, accident
- 예 *The earthquake was a catastrophe.*

declaration [dèkləréiʃən]   *n.* 선언

- 图 a formal public statement
- 图 announcement, proclamation, pronouncement, annunciation, statement
- 예 *a declaration of independence*

fasten [fǽsn]   *vt.* 고정하다

- 图 cause to be firmly attached
- 图 bind, tie, fix, attach, secure
- 예 *Fasten the lock onto the door.*

squeeze [skwíːz]   *vt.* 짜내다

图 compress with violence, out of natural shape or condition

图 squash, crush, squelch, mash, compress

예 *To make lemonade, queeze a lemon firstly.*

---

stuff [stʌf]   *n.* 물건, 사물

图 the tangible substance that goes into the makeup of a physical object

图 material, substance, matter, goods, objects, effects

예 *Wheat is the stuff which bakers use to make bread.*

---

*Vocabulary/Expressions

---

excursion [ikskə́:rʒən]   *n.* 소풍

㊊ a journey taken for pleasure

㊌ expedition, tour, picnic, outing, jaunt, ramble, trip

㊀ *We will go on an excursion to the East Sea.*

---

delinquent [dilíŋkwənt]   *a.* 체납의

㊊ not paid at the scheduled time

㊌ overdue, outstanding, unpaid, owing

㊀ *a delinquent account*

---

endanger [indeindʒər]   *vt.* 위험에 빠뜨리다

㊊ pose a threat to

㊌ menace, imperil, jeopardize, threaten, menace, hazard

㊀ *The pollution is endangering the crops.*

---

harmful [háːrmfəl]   *a.* 유해한

㊊ causing or capable of causing harm

㊌ injurious, hurtful, calamitous, destructive, malicious

㊀ *harmful effects of smoking*

---

claim [kleim]   *vt.* 요구하다

㊊ demand as being one's due or property

㊌ require, need, challenge, call for, postulate

㊀ *He claimed his suitcases at the airline counter.*

---

cozy [kouzi]   *a.* 기분 좋은

㊊ having or fostering a warm or friendly and informal atmosphere

㊌ easeful, comfortable, snug, restful, comfy

㊀ *The small room was cozy and intimate.*

---

proprietor [prəpraiətər]　　　　　　　　　　*n.* (상점, 호텔 등의) 소유자

图 someone who owns (is legal possessor of) a business

동 master, holder, possessor, landlord, owner

예 *He is the proprietor of a chain of restaurants.*

---

retire [ritaiər]　　　　　　　　　　*vi.* 퇴직하다, 은퇴하다

图 stop performing one's work or withdraw from one's position

동 regress, retreat, repeal, recede, stop working

예 *He retired at age 68.*

---

periodical [piəriádikəl]　　　　　　　　　　*n.* 정기 간행물

图 a publication that appears at fixed intervals

동 journal, review, weekly, magazine, serial

예 *The company publishes a periodical.*

---

consolidate [kənsálədeit]　　　　　　　　　　*vi.* (토지·회사 등을) 합병 정리하다

图 unite into one

동 combine, unite, amalgamate, coalesce, merge, incorporate

예 *The companies consolidated.*

---

serious [síəriəs]　　　　　　　　　　*a.* 진지한

图 concerned with work or important matters rather than play or trivialities

동 austere, contemplative, earnest, solemn, pensive, sedate

예 *Are you serious or joking?*

---

notify [nóutəfài]　　　　　　　　　　*vt.* 통보하다

图 inform (somebody) of something

동 inform, advise, report, announce, mention, communicate

예 *I notified him that the rent was due.*

exempt [igzempt]   *vt.* 면제하다

图 grant relief or an exemption from a rule or requirement to

图 liberate, discharge, free, acquit, relieve, exonerate

예 *She exempted me from the exam.*

---

reservation [rezərveiʃən]   *n.* 예약

图 the act of reserving (a place or passage) or engaging the services of (a person or group)

图 preengagement, booking, appointment, precontract

예 *I wondered who had made the reservation.*

---

arrange [əréindʒ]   *vt.* 배열하다

图 put into a proper or systematic order

图 array, order, dispose, settle, organize

예 *Arrange the books on the shelves in chronological order.*

---

frightened [fràitnd]   *a.* 깜짝놀란

图 thrown into a state of intense fear or desperation

图 afraid, scared, terrified, fearful, dismayed

예 *The frightened horse bolted.*

---

dispose [dispóuz]   *vt.* 처리하다

图 throw or cast away

图 throw, chuck, discard, fling, toss

예 *Dispose your worries.*

---

fragile [frǽdʒəl]   *a.* 부서지기 쉬운

图 easily broken or damaged or destroyed

图 breakable, dainty, frail, brittle, weak, feeble

예 *fragile porcelain plates*

---

commit [kəmit] *vt.* 위탁하다, 맡기다

뜻 grant authority to undertake certain functions

동 entrust, delegate, intrust, empower, authorize

예 *I commit my soul to God.*

aisle [ail] *n.* 통로

뜻 passageway between seating areas as in an auditorium or passenger vehicle or

between areas of shelves of goods as in stores

동 passage, alley, gangway, corridor, passageway

예 *Walk down the aisle.*

prosecute [prásikjuːt] *vt.* 수행하다

뜻 carry out or participate in an activity

동 carry on, conduct, execute, continue, practice, perform

예 *She prosecuted many activities.*

compose [kəmpouz] *vt.* 구성하다

뜻 form the substance of

동 constitute, be made of, comprise, form, construct

예 *His personality is composed of greed and ambition.*

adequate [ǽdikwət] *a.* 충분한; 알맞은

뜻 sufficient for the purpose

동 sufficient, appropriate, fit, enough, suitable

예 *an adequate income*

benefit [bénəfit] *n.* 이익

뜻 something that aids or promotes well-being

동 advantage, favor, profit, avail, worth

예 *I worked hard for my benefit.*

stipulation [stipjulei∫ən]　　　　　　　　　　　　　　*n.* 약정, 계약

園 an agreement or concession made by parties in a judicial proceeding relating to the business before the court

類 contract, terms, engagement, arrangement, treaty

例 *A stipulation of fact was made in order to avoid delay.*

species [spíː∫iːz]　　　　　　　　　　　　　　　　　*n.* 종

園 a specific kind of something

類 class, sort, genus, type, kind

例 *a species of molecule*

overwhelming [òuvərhwélmiŋ]　　　　　　　　　*a.* 압도적인

園 so strong as to be irresistible

類 overpowering, amazing, intense, crushing, vast

例 *an overwhelming need for solitude*

clumsy [klʌmzi]　　　　　　　　　　　　　　*a.* 어색한, 서투른

園 not elegant or graceful in expression

類 unskilful, awkward, maladroit, incompetent, inept

例 *a clumsy prose style*

mutual [mjuːtʃuəl]　　　　　　　　　　　　　　*a.* 공통의

園 common to or shared by two or more parties

類 common, shared, public, connected, reciprocal

例 *the mutual interests of management and labor*

convention [kənven∫ən]　　　　　　　　　　　　*n.* 집회

園 a large formal assembly

類 assembly, conference, meeting, covenant

例 *political convention*

reference [réfərəns]   *n.* 참조

图 a short note recognizing a source of information or of a quoted passage

图 citation, mention, cite, quotation

예 *The article includes reference of similar clinical cases.*

---

postpone [poustpóun]   *vt.* 연기하다

图 hold back to a later time

图 put off, adjourn, delay, defer, suspend

예 *Let's postpone the exam.*

---

exertion [igzə́rʃən]   *n.* 노력, 진력, 분발

图 use of physical or mental energy; hard work

图 effort, travail, endeavor, struggle, toil

예 *They managed only with great exertion.*

---

decision [disíʒən]   *n.* 결정

图 a position or opinion or judgment reached after consideration

图 conclusion, ruling, determination, finding, verdict

예 *a decision unfavorable to the opposition*

---

fraction [frǽkʃən]   *n.* 파편

图 a small part or item forming a piece of a whole

图 part, fragment, portion, slice, piece

예 *fractions of broken glass*

---

relieve [rilíːv]   *vt.* 경감하다

图 lessen the intensity of or calm

图 alleviate, abate, ease, mitigate, soothe, assuage

예 *The news relieved my conscience.*

occupation [àkjupéiʃən]   *n.* 직업

園 principal activity in your life that you do to earn money

圖 job, metier, profession, vocation, career

圓 *The man was out of occupation.*

---

appraise [əpreiz]   *vi.* (물건·재산을) 값매기다, 견적을 내다

園 evaluate or estimate the nature, quality, ability, extent, or significance of

圖 judge, assess, valuate, price, measure

圓 *I will have the family jewels appraised by a professional.*

---

flatter [flǽtər]   *vi.* 아첨하다

園 praise somewhat dishonestly

圖 cajole, adulate, blandish, inveigle, butter up, wheedle

圓 *a flattering remark*

---

observation [àbzərveiʃən]   *n.* 관찰

園 the act of taking notice

圖 attention, notice, investigation, surveillance, perception, regard

圓 *observation deck*

---

chop [tʃáp]   *vt.* 자르다

園 cut into pieces

圖 cleave, lop, divide, hack, slash, fragment

圓 *Chopping wood is not difficult.*

---

supreme [səpri:m]   *a.* 최고의

園 highest in excellence or achievement

圖 paramount, sovereign, top, utmost, superlative

圓 *He is supreme among musicians.*

271

recession [riseʃən]

n. 경기후퇴

- 图 the state of the economy declines
- 图 bankruptcy, depression, retreat, decline, stagnation
- 예 *structural recession*

resolution [rèzəlú:ʃən]

n. 결정

- 图 the outcome of decision making
- 图 decision, settlement, determination, closure, verdict
- 예 *They never did achieve a final resolution of their differences.*

legislation [ledʒisleiʃən]

n. 법률

- 图 law enacted by a legislative body
- 图 constitution, lawact, commandment, order, regulation
- 예 *protective legislation*

startle [stá:rtl]

vt. 깜짝 놀라게 하다

- 图 move or jump suddenly, as if in surprise or alarm
- 图 surprise, alarm, scare, frighten, terrify
- 예 *She startled me when I walked into the room.*

alternate [ɔltərneit]

vi. 번갈아 하다

- 图 do something in turns
- 图 fluctuate, alter, shift, change, vacillate
- 예 *We alternate on the night shift.*

repeal [ripi:l]

vt. 무효로 하다

- 图 cancel officially
- 图 annul, cacel, nullify, abolish, invalidate, withdraw
- 예 *Please, repeal this death sentence.*

drizzle [drizl]   *vi.* 이슬비 내리다

뜻 rain lightly

유 mizzle, dribble, spit, mist, sprinkle

예 *When it drizzles in summer, hiking can be pleasant.*

---

impressive [impresiv]   *a.* 강한 인상을 주는

뜻 producing a strong effect

유 effective, influential, striking, imposing, vital

예 *He gave an impressive performance as Othello.*